Flying the Light
Retractables

Flying the Light Retractables

A guided tour through the most popular
complex single-engine airplanes

LeRoy Cook

Aviation Supplies & Academics, Inc.
Newcastle, Washington

Flying the Light Retractables
A guided tour through the most popular complex single-engine airplanes
by LeRoy Cook

About the Author: LeRoy Cook chose to become a lifelong student of aviation in his early years, catching the fever during the celebration of the 50th Anniversary of powered flight in 1953. He determined to learn and share as much of aviation as he could, and is still exploring flight 50-plus years later. His career as an aviation writer began in 1970; he had been a flight instructor since 1965 and wanted to reach a wider audience, through aviation publications. With over 1,350 magazine articles published, Cook was a monthly columnist at *Private Pilot Magazine* for 34 years, where he was a senior editor. He holds ATP ratings for single and multi-engine airplanes, with commercial glider and seaplane ratings and his Gold Seal flight instructor's certificate carries single and multi-engine airplane, instrument and glider privileges. A lifelong resident of western Missouri, Cook is married with three children and continues teaching others about flying on a daily basis.

Aviation Supplies & Academics, Inc.
7005 132nd Place SE
Newcastle, Washington 98059-3153
Email: asa@asa2fly.com
Internet: www.asa2fly.com

Published 2007 by Aviation Supplies & Academics, Inc.

All photography © LeRoy Cook

Printed in the United States of America

2010   2009   2008   2007   9   8   7   6   5   4   3   2   1

ASA-FLY-RG
ISBN 1-56027-607-X
       978-1-56027-607-4

Library of Congress Cataloging-in-Publication Data:

Cook, LeRoy.
    Flying the light retractables : a guided tour through the most popular complex single-engine airplanes / LeRoy Cook.
       p.   cm.
       ISBN-13: 978-1-56027-607-4 (pbk.)
       ISBN-10: 1-56027-607-X (pbk.)
    1. Airplanes—Piloting. I. Title.
     TL710.C685 2007
      629.132'5—dc22
                                    2007032392

Contents

Introduction

As young-in-experience pilots seek to expand their horizons beyond the local airport-hopping routes, the option of a high-performance airplane begins to loom large in their thinking. Because their needs have grown beyond trainers and entry-level four-placers, it's tempting to consider light retractable-gear airplanes, powered by 180 or 200-hp engines. These small four-seat aircraft offer gear-up pizzazz, speeds of 150-mph or more and the capability of easily making trips of 500 miles, with IFR (instrument flight rules) reserves. At the same time, a light retractable's 10 gallon per hour fuel burn is only slightly more than that of a pedestrian fixed-gear airplane.

Through the years, 180/200-hp light retractables have been a very popular class of airplane, with more choices than any other market niche. Not only did the big-three manufacturers consistently offer such airplanes, quite a few start-up designs were aimed at this segment of the market, notably the Mooney series and the Rockwell Commander 112. It is for the prospective buyer of these light retractables that this book was written; to spell out the choices, give details of specifications and production history and tell how each one flies. With few exceptions, all are out of production, and careful shopping is required to find just the right airplane for your needs.

Most of the light retractable aircraft were designed to be personal airplanes. That is, they are to be flown and managed as a family and business transport, on whatever mission the owner dictates, rather than as a corporate airplane flown by a company pilot and hangared at a full-service FBO. They are still small and economical enough to be cared for by one person; as with their fixed-gear cousins, the owners will be washing, changing oil, vacuuming out the interior and agonizing over the insurance and maintenance bills.

All of these airplanes share a common trait; their ability to pick up their feet to enhance performance. A performance increase can be gained in one of two ways; by going to a higher-horsepower engine or reducing aerodynamic drag. Light retractables pursue the latter course, using almost the same engine as in their fixed-gear compatriots but folding up their wheels cleanly, out of the slipstream. This philosophy is most evident in a comparison of the Cessna Skylane with the Piper Arrow; both will cruise in the 150 mph range, yet the fixed-gear Skylane uses a 470-cubic inch 230-hp Continental engine that burns 12 gallons per hour, while the Arrow gets by with a 360-cubic inch 200-horsepower Lycoming, sipping 10 gallons per hour.

In several cases, transition training is made easier by familiarity with similar fixed-gear airplanes; there are few added complications other than the gear switch and a propeller control to be mastered. The Piper Arrow's cockpit is strikingly similar to that of the Piper Archer; the door latching arrangement, window line, seating and baggage compartment, instrument placement, even the line-up of electrical switches—all are identical. This deja vu factor also exists with the Cessna Cutlass RG and Cardinal RG and the Beech Sierra, each of which shared a cockpit with a fixed-gear cousin.

Some light retractables stand alone, like the Mooney, Commander, Comanche and the unique Lake amphibian, although in the case of the first two there were plans to make cheaper, fixed-gear versions when the market was right. We will also take a look at older, low-horsepower retractables, such as the early Bonanzas. To make it easier to compare each of the light retractable-gear airplanes, we've gathered performance and specification data into an Appendix at the end of the book. The field of light retractables is an exciting one, and it's a fine way to step up to another level of performance.

1 · The Mooney Family

The Mother Church of Light Retractables

If there were a quintessential light retractable, it would have to be the Mooney M20 series, from the original Mark 20 to the M20J. As the first four-place retractable-gear airplane designed around the light, powerful Lycoming four-cylinder engine, the Mooney created a whole new class of efficient, personal traveling machines.

Using the prevailing standards of Civil Air Regulation Part 3, the Mooney M20 received its initial type certification on August 24, 1955; it is from this original TC that most variants have been certificated. Although the basic layout has remained the same, one will find that the newer Mooneys have very little in common with the first airplanes, in either construction methods or aircraft systems. Tracing the history of the Mooney Company will help us understand the evolution of the M20 series.

Al Mooney began his career in aircraft design in the mid-1920s, working for various other firms until the euphoric period after the end of World War II, when he and his brother Art started Mooney Aircraft Company in that hotbed of aviation, Wichita, Kansas. His first product was a tiny single seat speedster with retractable landing gear and flaps, dubbed the M18 Mooney Mite. Initially powered by a converted Crosley auto engine, producing all of 25 hp, the Mite was quickly retrofitted with 65-hp Lycoming and Continental engines. The M18 was built from 1946 through 1955, by which time the Mooneys had left the payroll of the company that bore their name. Mooney Aircraft moved from Wichita to Kerrville, Texas in 1953, as development of a new, larger Mooney was well underway.

A four-place Mooney M20 had been on Al Mooney's drawing board by mid-1952, resembling a scaled-up Mite. As with the M18, the first Mooney Mark 20s utilized truly composite construction; the wing was built entirely of wood, including a spruce plywood skin to minimize airflow disruption over the laminar-flow airfoil section. The empennage was also built of wood, while the fuselage used a combination of monocoque aluminum construction in the tailcone area and non-stressed aluminum skin over a tubular steel truss around the cabin area. The engine was Lycoming's brand-new 150-hp O-320,

Pre-1961 Mooney Mark 20As like this one had a wood wing and tail, although the fuselage was aluminum skinned. Most have now been retired.

tightly cowled and turning a Hartzell constant-speed propeller. The landing gear and flaps were manually operated.

The light, compact Mark 20, with an empty weight of only 1,415 pounds, exceeded the one-mph-per-horsepower standard by a considerable amount, reputedly cruising at 165 mph and hitting a 171 mph top speed. By 1957, Lycoming had its 180-hp O-360 engine ready, and it appeared in the 1958 Mark 20A with a McCauley constant-speed propeller; its maximum cruise speed was quoted at 180 mph, with a top speed of 190. Exhaust augmenter tubes under the belly of the original M20 did a good job of enhancing cooling airflow through the engine, but they produced a husky bark, causing adjustable cowl flaps and a conventional exhaust system to be fitted to the 1958 airplanes. Both the Mark 20 and Mark 20A were offered for 1958; the 180-hp airplane outsold its smaller brother by a three-to-one margin, so only the M20A was offered thereafter. In all, some 700 Mark 20 aircraft were built.

Years of neglect and outside storage have taken their toll on the 1955–1960 wood-construction Mooneys, some of which exhibited deterioration, particularly in the tail area. At this point, most of the wooden Mooneys have been converted to metal tails, at considerable cost, due to rigorous load tests required by a recurring AD to detect failures in the wooden tail structure.

By 1960 a market preference for all-metal aircraft was clearly evident, requiring the M20A to be redesigned with a metal wing and tail. Initial doubts about Mooney's ability to substitute flush riveting for smooth plywood were laid to rest, and the 1961 M20B appeared as the Mark 21, starting with serial #1701. A total of 48-gallons of fuel was now carried in integral wet-wing bays within the wing; the wood-wing Mooneys offered 35 gallons in the wings and an optional 14 gallons in an aft-fuselage tank. The Mark 21's flaps and landing gear were still manually operated; the wheels folded away with a hefty bar that moved through a 90° arc, from a vertical location under the panel to a flat position on the floor between the seats. The flaps, meanwhile, were extended by a small chrome lever under the panel that one pulled down to engage one of two notches. Empty weight increased by about 85 pounds with the conversion to metal construction, and the advertised cruise speed was boosted by 2 mph, to 182 mph. A total of 222 M20Bs were built.

For 1962, Mooney brought out its M20C, still marketed as the Mark 21. The most obvious changes were an increase in gross weight, from the earlier airplane's 2,450 pounds to 2,575 pounds, and the installation of a hydraulic hand-pump to lower the flaps, using the same handle as the M20B. A few strokes with the selector in the "down" position extended the flaps to as much as 33°, up from 21.5° in the M20B. Flipping the selector to "up" allowed the hydraulic pressure to bleed off, retracting the flaps. The M20C, as the basic 180-hp, carburetor-equipped economy Mooney, settled in for a long, stable production run, even while other permutations evolved; renamed the Ranger in 1965, it was still in production when the 201 was introduced in late 1976. The final 15 M20Cs were built in 1978, for a total of 2,192 airplanes.

The Mooney line was expanded in 1963 to include a fixed-gear, fixed-pitch entry-level version called the M20D Master. Maximum cruise speed was quoted as 139 mph, and gross weight was identical to the M20C, with 50 pounds more useful load. Because the airframe was identical to the Mark 21, the owner of an M20D could have it converted to a retractable-gear airplane at any time, as practically all have been by now. Only 161 Masters were built through 1966.

For 1964, new flush-fitting fuel filler caps replaced the old thermos-type caps under a hinged plate, increasing fuel capacity by four gallons. A Super 21

The 200-hp Mooney M20E Super 21 was one of the fastest small Mooneys, particularly when modified with a sleeker cowling and windshield, as this one has been. Stretched into the M20F Executive 21, it eventually became the M20J 201.

Some Mooneys may still be seen with an automotive-type shock absorber on the nosegear to limit rebound. Proper landing technique makes it unnecessary.

M20E, using Lycoming's new 200-hp IO-360-A1A fuel-injected four-banger, came along in 1964, expanding the line to three models. The hot-rod M20E proved to be the most popular version yet, selling at a 400 to 500 per year rate in the mid-60s; it was renamed the Chaparral in 1969, after a one year hiatus in 1968, and was built through 1975, for a total of 1,471 airplanes. Top speed was advertised as 197 mph, and cruise speed at 75% power was 187 mph, enhanced by a "ram air" feature that allowed the pilot to bypass the air filter to gain an extra inch of manifold pressure. The Super 21 routinely indicated well into the yellow arc, which began at 150 mph in airplanes built prior to 1969, after which the yellow arc was expanded to 175 mph and the flap limit speed was raised from 100 mph to 125.

Nineteen-sixty-five saw the introduction of Mooney's "PC" (positive control) feature, a full-time wing-leveler autopilot that could only be turned off by depressing a thumb-button on the pilot's control wheel. New square-edge cabin windows replaced the rounded window lines from the 1950s.

Electrically-operated landing gear was optional by 1966, for those who just couldn't master the bicep-building manual gear. The year 1966 also brought yet another significant new product; the M20F Executive, the first long-cabin Mooney. The extra few inches of aft-seat room gained by the Exec proved highly popular; the rear side windows were divided into two panes to play up the additional space. Sharing the M20E's powerplant, maximum cruise speed supposedly ranged up to 187 mph; in actual practice, 170 would be more typical. Gross weight was increased to 2,740 pounds, and fuel capacity was boosted to 64 gallons. The M20F was the airframe that was chosen to be metamorphosed into the M20J, or 201. Although it was certificated on July 25, 1965, production of the new Executive 21, as it was first known, didn't begin rolling in earnest until 1967, when 536 rolled out the factory door. A total of 1,241 Executives were built, forever eroding the short-cabin Super 21's market share by offering increased back-seat comfort.

In 1966 Mooney also fielded its first M22 Mustang, a five-place pressurized-cabin airplane that shared little of the M20-series other than the wing layout. The M22 is mentioned here only because of its deleterious effect on the company's health; the considerable expense of its development and below-cost pricing led to changes of ownership and rough times in the subsequent years. The Executive and Mustang ushered in the practice of beginning all serial numbers with the year of manufacture; by 1967 all models had adopted this numbering system.

Nineteen-sixty-eight saw the M20E dropped from the line, leaving only the M20C Ranger as a short-cabin airplane, but another new model was introduced, the M20G Statesman. The M20G combined the Executive 21's long-cabin airframe with the Ranger's 180-hp carburetor-equipped engine, a combination fated to result in lackluster performance; it was supposed to be just 10 mph slower than an Executive and about 4 mph faster than a Ranger. In practice, its 2,525 pound gross weight tipped the scales to the favor of the Ranger's parentage. The Statesman was a good, solid airplane that failed to find its market niche; it was built for only three years, with 189 produced.

A new panel and quadrant-style power controls were introduced in 1969, and electrically-operated landing gear was made standard. Sixty-nine also brought back the short-cabin, big-engine M20E, now named the Chaparral, giving Mooney a complete line of engine and airframe combinations. However, continued slow sales led to a shutdown of production in 1971, when only the Ranger, Chaparral and Executive were built in limited quantities. The factory was to lie moribund for over two years, other than for parts fabrication.

In October 1973, ownership passed to Republic Steel, which brought a badly-needed measure of stability to the company during the next 10 years; in 1984, ownership passed to Eurlair, a French charter company. Mooney resumed limited production on January 1, 1974 and a total of 140 airplanes were built in 1974, with 186 rolling out the following year, divided among M20C, M20E and M20F models. A new instrument panel, control yoke and power quadrant knobs were introduced in mid-1975. Only the M20C short-cabin economy airplane and M20F long-cabin 200-hp version were built in 1976, as the M20E short-cabin 200-hp airplane was dropped from the line.

Big things were happening, however. Roy LoPresti had been brought in from Grumman American to work miracles similar to those he had wrought with Grumman's AA-5 Traveler. Under his direction, the M20F Executive was given an aerodynamic cleanup that resulted in an increase in top speed to 201 mph—the M20J, called the Model 201 for its maximum speed, was born, just in time for the 1977 model year (there was no production of an M20H). Only

Seen from the side, a Mooney 201 inflight shows why it's so fast; everything possible has been tucked away or faired into the slipstream.

This 1978 Mooney 201 shows the transition from Mooney's use of truncated wingtips and the shock absorber on the nosewheel, to the later models as shown by the M20J MSE photo on page 20.

7 Executives built in 1977, but a whopping 377 201s rolled out the door. In 1978 Mooney kept up the pace, cranking out another 380 201s, along with the last 15 of the M20C Rangers.

As a marketing move, Mooney redesignated the M20J as the 205 in mid-1987, to advertise a slight additional gain in top speed from refinements developed for the M20K 231. The airplanes received a rounded window shape to give them a distinctive new look. Mooney returned to the 201 designation in 1989, and also introduced a bold new M20L Mooney PFM, a stretched airframe with a Porsche six-cylinder, 193-cubic-inch, geared, fan-cooled engine capable of producing 217 horsepower. While the highly-automated Porsche powerplant was much simpler to operate than a Lycoming or Continental engine (no mixture control, no propeller control, no cowl flaps), its offshore origin, extra cost and added weight made it unattractive to established airplane owners and it was never discovered by its main market, new first-time buyers who wanted to avoid high-performance hassles. The PFM sold poorly, if at all, and was discontinued after 1990. The rest of the Mooney line had also undergone replacement of model numbers with three-letter designations; the 201 became the 201SE, then the MSE, and the M20K was dubbed the TSE.

In 1989, the hulking M20M TLS appeared, powered by a big 270-hp Lycoming TSIO-540 powerplant turning a three-blade propeller. It quickly became the flagship of the Mooney fleet, and by 1999 Mooney discontinued production of all small-engine airplanes in favor of the long-fuselage, large engine models.

The *real* Mooney, however, remains the 180/200-hp normally-aspirated four-placer, exactly the market in which Al Mooney had intended his M20 to compete. The thousands of airframes out there generate a vast field of potential used equipment, giving plenty of choices for buyers. In general, if you have need of carrying four persons you'll want to shop for a long-cabin model, such as the Executive, Statesman or 201. If, on the other hand, you're flying mostly one or two-up and primarily seek cross-country speed at minimal cost, you can pick from a wide selection of M20C or M20Es, in addition to the longer airplanes. We'll give examples of long-and-short Mooney airplanes to show how the M20 series was constructed and how they fly.

2 · Flying an Early Mooney M20C

As we said in the chapter on Mooney history, it was Lycoming's development of a 150-hp four-cylinder engine in the early 1950s that made practical Al Mooney's concept of an efficient four-seat traveling airplane. This basic powerplant had the growth potential to put out 180–200 hp and was particularly useful when coupled to one of Hartzell's lightweight constant-speed propellers. The Mooney Mark 20 was certificated in August of 1955, but the airplane's wood wing and tail, as inherited from the single-place M18 Mite, contributed to the slow pace of sales in the beginning. When a redesigned all-metal version, the M20B Mark 21, was introduced in 1961, the now-180-hp Mooney was on its way to success; the M20B received certification on December 14, 1960.

The follow-on M20C, certificated on October 20, 1961, became one of the most popular Mooney models, remaining in the line-up through 1978, by

Despite some modifications to the nosecap and spinner, this 1963 Mooney M20C has the lines and look of a basic Mooney, the foundation of a line of popular light retractables.

which time 2,192 examples had been built. The -C model sired an entire line of progeny, from the 200-hp M20E Super 21 to the stretched M20J 201.

An M20D that Became an M20C

But what of that -D model, between the M20C and -E, the fixed-gear Mooney Master that was to be bought and flown by entry-level owners and then converted at minimal cost and confusion into retractable-gear M20Cs? Practically the entire lot has been absorbed into the ranks of -C models, including the fine example we've used for this chapter.

Originally built as a fixed-gear Mooney Master M20D, this sharp-looking early Mooney was converted to a retractable M20C; the longest-produced model in the Mooney family. It was also one of the last to be built with the original Mooney's arched window line. Powered by a simple carburetor-equipped 180-hp Lycoming O-360, it has manually-operated landing gear.

Our test airplane was owned by Russ Barnett of Springfield, Missouri, who had been flying for over 4 decades and had definite ideas about what his personal traveling airplane should be. He and his enthusiastic wife Becky roamed the country in their magic carpet, N6646U, a well-appointed M20D/C. We were drawn to the Barnett airplane because, while outfitted with numerous enhancing modifications, it preserved the flavor of the early Mooneys. Built in 1963, it featured the last year of the rounded side-window shape; 1964 introduced a straight window line.

The Barnett airplane also had the remarkable manual landing gear actuating lever (please, please, don't call it a "Johnson Bar," which was a 1930s braking apparatus), and yet its flaps were hydraulically-extended by a hand pump, an improvement over the limited-travel two-notch manual flaps used through 1961. There was even a retractable boarding step to cut drag, like the pre-1960s Bonanzas, except Mooney pilots raised and lowered their step with 2.5 turns of a hand crank while the Bonanza's was linked to the gear.

Forever Features

Mooney uses pushrods throughout for control linkages: there are no cables and pulleys to get out of rig. The famous "backwards" tail has a straight-up leading edge and forward-swept trailing edge, and the whole assembly tilts for pitch trim, adjusting stabilizer incidence instead of stealing knots by deflecting a trim tab. If you want to see another example of this efficient design, check out a Lockheed JetStar business jet. The Mooney wing is made in one piece, with a continuous spar from tip to tip, thus the fuselage rests atop the wing. A load-carrying chromoly steel tube roll cage surrounds the cabin, and the trailing-link landing gear is sprung by rubber-biscuit cushions. The baggage compartment door swings upward out of the way, offering 120 pounds of capacity. Every one of these features from 1963 was still being used in brand-new Mooneys built 40 years later. If it ain't broke, don't fix it…

The Barnetts pointed out some of the added touches that made Four-Six Uniform their personal plane. A one-piece windshield improved visibility and a sleek spinner and nosecap from Air Resources International picked up several knots. Underneath, the maingear wheel wells had been closed in with

Mooney's classic tail pivots in its entirety for pitch trim; the diagonal seam in the vertical fin above the horizontal tail's leading edge allows free movement. All controls are pushrod operated.

liners, the brakes were relocated to get them out of the air stream and flap gap seals were installed to compliment the control surface gap seals Mooney always used. Because the lower-cost M20D Master didn't have a dorsal fin or a streamlining fillet at the stabilizer's juncture, they were installed to complete the M20C transition; wing root fairings were added as well.

Aft of the big -J model style spinner and tight cowling, opening the oil access door to the engine compartment reveals a snug snake pit of accessories, including the firewall-mounted 12-volt battery. Cowl flaps are provided, but even with them open Barnett says the engine still runs slightly warm in a V_Y climb due to his cowling mods.

The stout Mooney gear uses rubber discs in compression for shock absorption.

The fuel system consists of two integral tanks, carrying 24 gallons in each wing; the capacity was increased to 26 gallons in 1964. The laminar-flow wing section is sensitive to airflow disruption, hence the use of flush riveting and up to .050 skin thickness. The skins are wrapped around the wing in a continuous sheet to avoid spanwise seams. Even the fuel filler caps are concealed beneath flush-fitting covers. The wing uses an NACA 63_2–215 airfoil at the root, modified to 64_1–412 at the tip; it had stall strips on both leading edges to assure a recognizable stall, beginning inboard. The pitot tube was under the left wing while dual yoked static ports were on the aft fuselage sides.

Entering a Personal Space

The Barnetts, like most Mooney owners, left the flaps partially extended to make sure heedless passengers don't tread on the "no step" legend emblazoned across the flap. We slipped into the cockpit for a look at a typical owner's personal space. Sure enough, Russ and Becky had pens and pencils stuck in corners and the checklists and charts were close at hand. In fact, everything in a Mooney M20C cockpit is close at hand, quite cozy and tidy. Boarding follows a specific order; pilot first, then copilot, both of whom roll their seats forward by grasping the windshield brace bar until their knees disappear under the

The short-body Mooney interior will hold four people—if they like each other enough. The front seats roll forward after being occupied, giving more leg room for the rear seats.

The early Mooney panel was arranged for ease of mounting; standard instrument placement had yet to be devised. The crank on the left sidewall retracts the boarding step; black-handled lever under panel is the manual gear lever, smaller chrome lever is the pump for the hydraulic flaps.

panel, thereby opening up space for the rear passengers to step in. Properly done, there actually is room for all.

The avionics package was very complete, but even so, N6646U didn't come out too badly, weight-wise. Empty tare was 1,643 pounds, so with full tanks the airplane could still haul 644 pounds in the cabin.

The early-60s controls arrangement placed the mixture knob between the throttle and prop controls, not unusual for the time. Instrument arrangement was likewise based on convenience of installation; the "standard T" was yet to be adopted. Right-hand brakes were not normally installed in 1963, so the occupant of Four-Six Uniform's left seat was automatically the pilot in command.

Starting procedure is typical for a low-wing carbureted engine; mixture rich, boost pump on, pump the throttle once or twice and engage the starter. After the big pistons sent a shudder through the diminutive airframe, we were idling smoothly, so we retracted the flaps and boarding step and proceeded to the runway. Mooneys have a fairly wide turning radius of 41 feet without braking, as there's but 14 degrees of nose gear steering. The ride is firm on the rubber-cushioned gear and the short wheelbase leads to some hobby-horse rocking.

The pretakeoff checklist is extensive, because the M-20C is a complex airplane, despite its size. Cowl flaps are rechecked open, the wing flaps are pumped to 15 degrees and stabilizer trim is rotated to takeoff, using indicators found on the center pedestal. Fuel selection should be on the fullest tank, but the selector is now under the pilot's seat, out of sight, so it's necessary to set the parking brake and roll the seat back to verify the valve. If the baggage door needs to be checked for latching it's an easy reach to push on it. The cabin door does not have a spring catch, requiring a positive action to hold it shut while rotating the latch; this is so you won't take off with it unfastened, which would require a return for landing. Even though the airplane flies normally with a trailing door, the slipstream forces make closing it in-flight impossible. Run-up is conducted at 1,700 rpm for magnetos, carburetor heat, propeller and systems checks. There is a red arc from 1,900 to 2,350 rpm that must be avoided for continuous operation.

Good to Go

Boost pump goes on, required as a precaution for takeoff and landing, and we're good to go. Under full power, the M20C moves out smartly and is quickly past 60 mph, where we lift the nose to break ground at 70 mph in about 900 feet of runway. The gear is best brought up quickly, before airspeed builds; if properly lubricated, the bar swings aft from the panel and latches flat on the floor with a quick, fluid movement. The trick is to grasp the handle with your hand rotated thumb-down so your wrist can rotate for maximum leverage as the bar moves past your hip. Flaps come up at 90 mph and the V_Y

Despite some modifications to the nosecap and spinner, this 1963 Mooney M20C has the lines and look of a basic Mooney, the foundation of a line of popular light retractables.

of 110 yields 800 fpm of climb. However, Barnett prefers to cruise-climb at 140 mph on 2500 rpm and full throttle, which gave us 500 fpm and improved engine cooling and visibility.

Leveling off at 3,500 feet MSL, hardly the airplane's best altitude (Barnett had flown it to nearly 19,000 feet!), we set the power at 24 squared, snugged the cowl flaps closed and confirmed the boost pump had been turned off as we left the pattern. The airspeed rose into the yellow arc above 150 mph, a not-unusual characteristic for older Mooneys until the V_{NO} was raised to 175 in 1970. The IAS settled on 162 mph, for a true airspeed of 174 mph on 9.2 gph. Handling at speed is solid and stiff; Mooneys are stable on the gauges and are best suited to boring straight ahead, quickly and efficiently. The pushrod controls have not a hint of slop in their linkage and there's only a short throw in the wheel between extremes of travel.

Barnett recalled cruising in formation with a Beech Sierra on a group trip, which required him to use 17 inches MP (about 50% power) producing a fuel burn of only 7 gph. We tried it and got an indicated speed of 125 mph, for a TAS of 134. Experimenting with a clean stall, the warning sounded at 70 mph and a good break was seen at 65. We then levered the gear into place (the normal and emergency gear extension procedures are the same, in case you wanted to know…) and pumped the flaps down to 33 degrees, which delayed the stall warning to 65 mph and the benign break to 58. Recovery was immediate.

Bringing It Home

The clean, long-wing Mooney is a great glider, so one has to plan arrivals well in advance. We reduced power to about 14 inches while still 3 miles from the field, which brought us to the 120-mph gear-operating speed as we hit the pattern. Flaps can go down below 100 mph, and we flew the pattern at 90 initially, slowing to 85 as we turned final, where the flap handle was pumped solid. Holding 80 mph over the fence, we were careful not to let the laminar-flow wing fully stall before we rolled the maingear onto the pavement, avoiding a thumpdown arrival. One must not enter the low-slung Mooney's strong ground effect with extra speed, which will cause floating. The 2,500-foot turnoff was made with little braking.

The 180-hp carbureted Mooneys are still prized and trade for several times their original selling price. Even as they near 50 years of age, they certainly don't show their age. To see what 30 years of tweaking does to the Mooney airframe, we'll compare the M20C to a late-model M20J.

3 · **Modern Classic**
Mooney's M20J 201/MSE

During the mid-1970s, rumors leaking out of Mooney Aircraft's Kerrville, Texas factory hinted at a 200-mph version of the Executive 21, the long-cabin Mooney that was introduced in 1967. Some observers speculated that it would use a huge (by Mooney standards) six-cylinder Lycoming engine; others alluded to a radical aerodynamic redesign.

On September 27, 1976, the new M20J received its FAA certification, and the rumors were laid to rest. It was dubbed the model 201, a marketing ploy that made sure everyone could quote the airplane's wide-open top speed in miles-per-hour. As a highly refined version of the basic M20 airframe, the new J-bird recaptured the efficiency crown for which Mooney had long been famous, using the same 200-hp IO-360 Lycoming engine employed by the Executive. Clean-up artist Roy LoPresti managed to squeeze 20 mph more speed out of the airframe without adding horsepower.

Mooney's first four-placers, fitted with a sleek wooden wing and tail, were capable of meeting the fabled one-mph-per-hp benchmark, but when production shifted to an all-aluminum airframe in 1961, certain efficiencies were compromised and a bit of speed slipped away due to the inevitable rivets, lap seams, antennas and hinges. The introduction of the longer M20F Executive 21 in 1967 improved cabin comfort, but further deteriorated cruise speed, in actual use if not in the brochure. Before the 201 was introduced, the 200-hp stretched Mooneys would cruise at an honest 165 mph, although 179 mph was the official max-cruise figure.

Much of the factory's work originally needed to create the M20J from the M20F took place forward of the cabin; the Executive's battering-ram windshield was changed to a more-sloping version, and the wide-open aluminum cowling was replaced by a tightly-contoured fiberglass nose bowl. Further aft, a long picture window replaced the two smaller windows beside the Executive's rear seat. The open main gear wells were partially covered by fairing doors attached to the wheels, and a streamlining afterbody under the wing smoothed airflow around the retracted tire. Other tweaking by LoPresti's drag reduction team at Mooney included flush riveting the underside of the wing forward of the spar, adding fairing covers for the protruding control hinges and drains and flush-mounting the side windows.

A New Plane for a New Age

Suddenly, the 201 was the airplane everyone wanted; it offered a 195-mph max cruise speed and, as its name implied, could nudge past 200 mph wide open. Mooney's timing couldn't have been better; the 1974 oil crisis was still a fresh memory and going fast on a miserly four-cylinder Lycoming seemed the sensible thing to do. It was a time for smaller cars, turned-down thermostats and solar heating. The snug little Mooney cabin suddenly took on an appeal far beyond its usual constituency, the hard-core Mooney devotees. Now Skylane and Lance pilots were switching to the fast, thrifty 201.

For a brief period in 1987 and 1988, the M20J was marketed as the "205SE," essentially a further refinement of the 201 with a few more knots of speed. To the buyer, however, it was still a "201," and the company reverted to the original designation for 1989, with the suffix SE, eventually switching to MSE in compliance with company policy to use letters instead of numbers. Whatever it was called, the little normally-aspirated speedster dominated the light-retractable market as soon as it appeared, so much so that most competitors fell by the wayside. About 2,150 M20Js were built through 1998, when production ended in favor of the six-cylinder models.

Periodic improvements continued to be added to the 201, even as it was sweeping the market. Maximum gear-extension speed was raised by 30 mph in 1978, from 120 mph to 150 mph (retrofittable to 1977 models), and a crank-down emergency gear-extension system was changed to a lawnmower-type pull cable that same year. The throttle, propeller and mixture controls were also returned to push-pull knobs in 1978, after the first year used the fake multi-engine quadrant from pre-201 Mooneys. A fiberglass dorsal fin with an improved ventilation airscoop was added in mid-1979, and the upswept low-drag wingtips of the M20K turbocharged 231 replaced the original square Mooney tips at serial number 1038 in 1981.

A one-piece fiberglass belly pan for quicker maintenance access and less drag was introduced in 1984, the most significant year in terms of the 201's enhancement. That year also saw the introduction of sealed nose gear doors to lessen drag and noise, a flush-fitting oil access door, high speed nav and ADF antennas and smaller two-inch power instruments. The 1986 201 LM "Lean Machine" returned to the 3-inch tachometer, however, as a low-cost model.

The 1987 M20J ("205") incorporated such changes as a 28-volt electrical system, electrically actuated, infinitely-adjustable cowl flaps, pre-select wing flaps with 15 degrees of extension permitted at speeds up to 132 knots, inner gear doors to completely enclose the wheels and another increase in gear speeds, up to 140 knots for extension and 165 knots after the wheels were down. Rounded windows were also added, to set the 205 apart from earlier M20Js.

As the ultimate M20J, the 1990's MSE version had a gross weight of 2,900 pounds, up from 2,740 pounds for the 201/205. Dual landing lights were in the wing leading edges (both sides) instead of the 201's single cowling-mounted light and the old ram-air induction hole was gone. Power boost, as it was called when it was introduced in the late 1960s, had given a bit more manifold pressure to the 200-hp Mooneys at altitude, but not enough to warrant keeping an extra control in the cockpit. The MSE remains a crowning achievement of 40 years of Mooneys with 361-cubic inch engines, which means it's now highly sought-after; only 287 were built during the difficult times of the '90s. For our sample airplane, we were fortunate to find a nice 1991 MSE, owned by Dianne and Tim White, two husband and wife pilots from Wichita, Kansas.

The Whites were justifiably proud of their efficient, well-equipped personal airliner. As we walked up to it on the ramp, the impression was one of sleekness, reinforced when we saw it in an air-to-air view with the gear tucked up and cowl flaps closed. Mooneys are dart-like slivers of airplane, tailored for their mission. Note the unbroken lines from spinner tip to cowling contours and over the sloped windshield. The cowl inlets are tight and even the exhaust pipe is faired in for clean cruise. Extra catches make sure the oil door stays sealed to keep cooling-air from leaking out of the upper cowling. The cowling is removable in sections, with screwdriver-twist fasteners.

In flight, the Mooney J-bird proudly wears its "backwards" tail, minimizing trim drag. Everything that can't be tucked away is heavily faired to slip through the air cleanly. A top speed of more than 200 mph on a 200-hp engine was the goal and the 201/205/MSE met that standard.

The MSE was built from 1990 to 1998, at the end of production for four-cylinder Mooneys. Note the upswept wingtips and lack of a shock absorber on the nosegear, compared to the early 201.

As with the M20C, the legendary single-piece laminar-flow wing has a stall strip on each leading edge to assure a consistent stall. The landing lights are at mid-span and a pitot tube is under the left wing, with static ports on the sides of the tailcone. If a slaved compass system is installed, the magnetic flux gate will usually be mounted in the left wingtip. Flap hinges are faired and the retracted flap meets a Teflon seal. The swooping wingtips incorporate recessed red/green position lights, strobe lights and aft-facing white position lights. So efficient is the wing that the M20J possesses an 11.46:1 glide ratio with the propeller windmilling in high pitch.

The MSE's 66.5 gallons of fuel are contained in integral bays, yielding 64 usable gallons, enough to outlast most pilots. External sight gauges in the upper wing skin were made standard in 1981 to facilitate partial fuel loading and there's a 25-gallon marker in each filler neck. According to the handbook, the sight gauges are not to be used by the preflighting pilot, only by the line crew adding fuel. Tank sump and gascolator drains are part of the duck-walk ritual, and there are also drains for the pitot and static lines, under the left wingroot and aft fuselage.

The rubber-disc trailing-link landing gear is an eternal design, but the M20C's manual actuation was eventually replaced by an effortless electric motor in the late 1960s. Because of the limited travel of its shock absorption, conventional squat switches wouldn't work, so Mooney devised an airspeed-actuated safety lockout for the gear motor, preventing it from running below 65 knots unless a bypass button is held in. For the MSE, emergency extension is by a ratchet-type cable and handle between the seats, rather like starting a chainsaw. The overlapping maingear doors shuffle like a deck of cards to nearly enclose the retracted gear, hiding brakes and gear legs out of the wind. An automotive-type shock absorber on the early 201 nosegear, a carryover from the airplane's 1955 certification, was deemed unnecessary in mid-1981 and was no longer used after that.

The baggage bin aft of the rear seats is reached through an upward-hinging door on the right side of the fuselage. The Mooney fuselage incorporates a steel truss surrounding the cabin area, visible as brace tubing in the center of the windshield and necessitating the high baggage door location. Thus, heavy suitcases have to be hoisted to shoulder height to clear the longerons. The baggage compartment holds 120 pounds, with another 10 pounds allowed on the extended hat shelf in the tailcone. The MSE's 24-volt battery is in the rear fuselage. A vent inlet on the dorsal fin feeds the overhead fresh air system. As with all Mooneys, the empennage pivots as a unit, vertical fin and horizontal stabilizer together, to adjust pitch trim. The pilot moves the gap-sealed tail control surfaces by pushrods, giving the traditional tight Mooney feel. No, say Mooney devotees, the tail is not on backwards; it's everyone else who slopes their tailfeathers the wrong way.

Built near the end of Mooney's production of light retractables, the MSE was an upgraded 201; both were M20J models. The MSE, however, used wing-mounted landing lights and had no ram-air induction opening.

Mooney's strength was always its ability to personalize airplanes to the owners' taste, such as the lavish avionics in this MSE. An all-electric airplane, the M20J has electric gear, wing flaps, cowl flaps and trim.

Captain's Quarters

We strode onto the beefy fixed step to mount the MSE's wingwalk, carefully avoiding the don't-tread-on-me flap skin, and opened the door to enter the luxurious leather-lined interior. Mooney cabins became steadily more sybaritic over the years as buyer expectations rose, and Three-five-Zulu's was quite well-appointed. When the M20E's cabin was given its 10-inch stretch to create the M20F that in turn begat the M20J, the living space got its most useful boost in Mooney's evolution. In addition to a lengthened interior, the M20F's wing was moved 5 inches aft to maintain balance, giving a better downward view compared to the M20C and E.

Mooney owners have always doted on their panels; even factory-installed radar was squeezed in at one point. Typically, the Whites had an extensive radio package installed; a BFG Stormscope, Garmin GNS-530 and GTX-320, and a full compliment of Bendix/King goodies including a KAP 150 autopilot with slaved HSI. As equipped, there was nearly 1,000 pounds of useful load, 594 of which was payload with tanks topped.

Door closure is done with the secret handshake of Mooney owners; don't slam it, just pull it shut and then rotate the latch. Roll the seat up with the windshield brace bar's assistance, then move it forward a bit more to make sure you have brake access. Mooneys are worn, like your favorite pair of jeans, rather than ridden, and are quite comfortable once you're settled in. Starting requires the usual injected-Lycoming checklist, except the M20J asks for both boost pump to be off and mixture to be out after boosting up some fuel pressure. Twisting and pushing the key engages the starter and the mixture goes rich after you're off and running. The MSE incorporates an excellent 13-station annunciator panel that warns of things like a hung starter, low fuel state and boost pump left on.

Avionics testing underway, we rolled off the ramp with direct nosegear steering, supplemented by toe brakes for those tight corners; the M20J's un-aided turn radius is relatively wide at 41 feet. The front seats have vertical height adjustment to help see over the glareshield. At runway end, we idled at 1,200 rpm for electrical generation, checked controls, set the wing flaps to 15-degrees for takeoff and verified cowl flaps open. Magnetos and propeller are checked at 2,000 rpm, since the yellow arc on the tachometer reads between 1,500 and 1,950 rpm.

Boost pump and strobes on, we rolled for takeoff and found that the glider-like Mooney wing goes to work early—using about 1,200 feet of runway to liftoff at 65 knots. Once past 75 knots the flaps come up and the quick-acting gear is retracted before its 107-knot stowing limit, normally not a problem. Best rate of climb comes at 89 knots; 1,000-fpm is seen at full power and a normal 100-knot cruise climb produces 700 fpm on 26-square power. V_X with flaps at 15° happens at 66 knots.

Moving On Out

Scooting rapidly up to 4,000 feet, where warm temperatures gave a density altitude of nearly 6,000 feet, we leveled off, closed the cowl flaps and tuned the engine for 70% power at 24-square. This generated an indicated airspeed of a solid 140 knots, a true airspeed of 152 knots (175 mph) on 9.8 gallons per hour. Reducing power to 23 inches at 2,400 rpm, about 65% power, yielded a true airspeed of 150 knots on 9.2 gph and a 60% setting at 21.5 inches gave a TAS of 144 knots, using only 8.6 gph.

The MSE does its best work between 6,000 and 8,000 feet, where Tim White says he can depend on 160 knots at 75% power, even better in cool weather. Fuel burn at 75% will run about 11 gph, he says, and if one steps up to a higher altitude to catch a tailwind the fuel flow drops back to less than 10 gph. A Mooney moves on rails at full cruise stride, with the short-stroke control travel stiffening up with speed. It is made to run, far and fast, and it makes fewer demands when hand-flown on instruments than most high-performance airplanes.

Slowing the MSE down for stalls takes determination, owing to the clean Mooney airframe, but not as much as with the earlier models; maximum gear-

After discontinuing its 200-hp light retractables, Mooney Aircraft concentrated on the stretched-fuselage six-cylinder models. Many purists insist that the M20J series, as represented by this MSE, was the finest balance of speed, efficiency and payload.

lowering speed is 140 knots, approach flaps can go out at 132 knots and one must wait for 115 knots to extend full flaps. Slow flight at 60 knots with gear and flaps down still gave reasonable control response. In dirty configuration, we heard a power-off stall warning at 55 knots and a benign break occurred at 50 or so. Cleaned up, the horn came on at 62 knots and the stall was found at 55, again with no untoward wing drop or control loss.

Returning for the inevitable landing, the well-organized Mooney pilot will endeavor to level off well away from the traffic pattern, trimming away airspeed to meet limit speeds and fly the pattern at 100 knots or less. A 90-knot base should be adjusted to 75 knots on final, and any excess speed needs to be dissipated prior to entering ground effect, where the long Mooney wing will use it against you in prolonged float. No attempt must be made to force the wheels on before reaching a proper landing attitude; the rubber gear will porpoise on impact, usually inviting an out-of-synch correction. Done right, the MSE is easy to land; we turned off in 1,500 feet, after an easy nose-high touchdown.

The areas of caution to be observed when shopping for a used Mooney 201 are varied. The chief concern is corrosion in the sidewall fuselage tubing of some early airplanes, frequently from moisture leakage around the cabin windows, which soaks sound-deadening insulation lying in contact with the steel tubing. There have actually been cases of so much water accumulating inside the tubes that they froze up and burst. The inspection and repair is outlined in Mooney Service Bulletin 208; a better sealant seems to be the answer to the water problems, found most often in the 1977 and 1978 models. Check for towing damage to the nosegear structure from exceeding turn limits, and the undersides of the wings should be closely inspected for fuel stains, as tank sealant deteriorates on older Mooneys.

As the epitome of small-engine Mooneys, an M20J 201, 205 or MSE is great personal transportation, offering speeds equal to airplanes with 50% more horsepower in what is usually a well-equipped package. If you find it a bit confining, be assured that you won't have to sit there for long. As we will see in the forthcoming chapters, however, there are many other light retractable options.

4 · The Bonanza's Beginning
Before There Was A Mooney…

Lest we leave you with the impression that the concept of a low-horsepower four-seat retractable originated with Mooney's M20 series, we should touch on the airplanes of an earlier time. Ten years before Mooney's little Lycoming-powered speedsters were introduced, a three-way competition had developed between Beech's Bonanza, North American's Navion and Bellanca's Cruisair. These airplanes were powered by six-cylinder engines of 150–185 hp and delivered state-of-the-art performance for the times.

While more suited for the collector or classic airplane buff because their restoration and upkeep requires considerable dedication, these airplanes do represent early attempts to market light retractables and are worthy of study, if only for comparison purposes. Accordingly, we will profile the most successful and familiar of them, the Beechcraft Bonanza.

A contemporary of the early Bonanza, the wood-and-fabric Bellanca Cruisair was powered by a 150-hp Franklin engine, later upgraded to a 190-hp Lycoming in the Cruisemaster.

The North American Navion beat the Bonanza to the postwar market, but couldn't compete. Early examples had the E-185 Continental engine, although most have been upgraded like this tip-tank equipped example.

Early Beech Bonanzas, those built from 1947 to 1956, were a far different airplane from their descendants with nearly twice the horsepower and half again the weight. As it was originally conceived, the Beechcraft Model 35 was a light, agile slip of an airplane, powered by an engine no more potent than that of our current four-place fixed-gear singles. The interior was plush by 1947 standards, but it now seems starkly Spartan in an age of supported vinyls and wood-look laminates. A fine balance of comfort, compactness and speed, the basic Bonanza capably filled its role of delivering high performance with efficiency, a combination that had been relatively unproven prior to its appearance.

Coming hard on the heels of an era of burly, radial-engine monoplanes and biplanes, the new Bonanza's sleek lines attracted the attention of dreamers and buyers everywhere. First flown in December of 1945, the airplane finally achieved certification on March 25, 1947. By that time, the demand for Bonanzas was frenetic, particularly at the low, low introductory price of $6,995. Prices quickly jumped to $7,975, then rose again to $8,945. In all about 1,500 of the first-edition "straight 35" Bonanzas were built in 1947 and 1948; these were replaced by the A35 in1949.

The Bonanza's most controversial feature was, of course, its unique V-tail, which combined elevator and rudder functions in only two moving surfaces. Less weight and drag was the touted reason for the butterfly tail, but its chief benefit was a distinct "signature" for the airplane. Nothing else looked like a Bonanza, and even though Beech never put another V-tail airplane into production, the Bonanza was a huge marketing success, and it remained so for 35 years and 10,000 units.

The Beech Bonanza model 35 looked fast just parked on the ground. This fully-restored 1947 Bonanza proudly represents the best of the early light retractables, before Beech Aircraft began a progression of power and weight increases.

Grossing at 2,550 pounds, the Model 35 was powered by a Continental E-185-1 six-cylinder engine producing 185 takeoff horsepower, turning a Beech-designed electrically controllable (not constant speed) propeller with wooden blades. Fully-retractable electric landing gear stowed under sequencing doors that opened and reclosed during the cycle to cut down on drag and mud accumulation. The maximum gear-extension speed was 125 mph, while the full 20 degrees of electric flaps could be deployed at no more than 100 mph IAS. Fabric-covered control surfaces were used at first, soon changed to magnesium skins. Fuel was carried in two bladder-type tanks in the leading edges of the wings, with 20 gallons in each tank providing only 17 gallons usable in all flight attitudes.

Chronological Evolution

Externally identical to the Model 35, the follow-on A35 of 1949 had a built-up aluminum carry through structure in the fuselage center section for the wing spar attachments, in place of the welded-steel truss used in the "straight 35." To remove some of the stigma associated with the allegedly lightweight center section of the original Bonanza, Beech won certification of the A35 in the utility category at a full gross weight of 2,650 pounds (unlike the Model 35's dual-category certification that provided a narrow utility envelope below 2,100 pounds). Flap limit speed was increased to 105 mph, and the

A35 featured a steerable nose wheel, rather than the unlamented swiveling unit of the Model 35 that relied on differential braking for steering.

The B35 was introduced for 1950, featuring an E-185-8 engine capable of producing 196 horsepower for takeoff, before reducing to the maximum continuous power of 165 hp. The B35 was the first Bonanza to offer all-over paint. Flap travel was increased to 30 degrees, with increased trim tab camber to aid control. A redesigned control wheel was installed, and a oil-access door was cut into the cowling as an alternative to raising the left half of the hinged upper cowl to check the oil.

A major change in the empennage occurred with the C35, when the dihedral angle of the ruddervators was increased to bring the "V" tail up to a higher angle. Corrugations were also added for stiffness and chord was increased. An E-185-11 engine offered 205 horsepower for takeoff and for the first time max-continuous power went up to 185 hp. A wing root fillet smoothed airflow at the fuselage juncture. Gross weight was increased to 2,700 pounds. The C35 was in production for 1951 and 1952.

The 1953 D35 received another slight gross weight increase to 2,725 pounds and separate reclining seats were introduced. The 1954 E35 offered a choice of the 205-hp -11 engine or the new E-225-8, yielding 225-hp for takeoff and 185 hp max-continuous power. The top of the green arc on the airspeed indicator was moved from 160 to 175 mph. By 1955 the F35 had increased skin thickness in the wing's leading edge, and gross weight went up to 2,750 pounds. The F35 also introduced small triangular rear windows above the baggage area, and it marked the first appearance of optional auxiliary fuel cells in the wings. With the fuel selector placed on "aux," fuel would feed from two ten-gallon cells simultaneously rather than from the baggage compartment tanks found in previous models.

The G35 for 1956 was the peak of lightweight Bonanza development. An E-225-8 engine was made standard, the windshield thickness was increased to 1/4 inch to quiet the cabin, and gross weight went up slightly to 2,775 pounds. Flap speed was increased to 120 mph and maximum gear-down speed became 140 mph.

Things were never the same after the G35. The 1957 model year was chosen to introduce a new, heavier, recertificated Bonanza, featuring a hydraulically-controlled constant-speed propeller, and a new Continental engine, its crankshaft drilled to supply the propeller with oil rather than the solid splined shaft of the E-series engines. The O-470-G produced 240 hp with no time limit, and it featured a wet-sump crankcase, as contrasted with the dry-sump E-series engine. The structure of the aircraft was beefed up to allow future growth, and the H35 received its own type certificate rather than an amendment to the 1947 Model 35's certification. All subsequent V-tail Bonanzas were certified under amendments to the H35's certificate.

The advent of the H35 erased forever the concept of a lightweight Bonanza; its gross weight was now 2,900 pounds, and the horsepower and cabin length would continue to grow until the final V35 series was begun in 1966, grossing out at 3,400 pounds. Speeds increased, both at cruise and at touchdown, and the fuel burn nudged 15 gph at high-cruise settings.

Fortunately, almost 5,000 of the pre-1957 Bonanzas were built, providing us with a plentiful supply of cases to study when shopping for a V-tail as an older light retractable. And study is required; the age of the early Beechcrafts means a careful eye must be kept out for corrosion, neglect and old damage that was poorly repaired. Beech's reputation for quality doesn't mean the airplanes are bulletproof, particularly if not maintained. Fortunately, the Bonanza's strengths and weaknesses are well known by now. The finest source of data will be found at the American Bonanza Society, headquartered at Wichita's Mid-Continent airport. Ownership is not a prerequisite for joining, so before buying it would be a good idea to send in your dues, read the newsletter and make use of the library available to ABS members.

Because the older Bonanza is a complex, high-performance aircraft, it will require expending a larger percentage of its value to maintain than simpler airplanes. Quite often, Bonanzas are sold not because of the need to tap an investment, but because the upkeep is taking too great a toll on the owner's income.

A great many of the early Bonanzas have been modified in some form or another, making it difficult to pin down a visual identification until checking the serial number. The blunt, two-piece windshields are commonly exchanged

Built in 1947, the "straight 35" Beech Bonanza pioneered the light-retractables concept. The low horsepower and gross weight, coupled with a sleek airframe, delivered more miles per gallon than the 240-285 hp Bonanzas produced after 1956.

for one-piece speed-slope extended designs, like that of the V35A. Tip tanks, with a legal increase in maximum takeoff weight, are a relatively easy way to supplement the 34 usable gallons in the mains (or even the 53 gallons of an aux-tank equipped bird). New panels with center stacked radios, M35-style wingtips, longer nose-gear doors, extended rear windows and baggage areas— all are popular mods that mask the age of the host airplane.

A Restored Classic

Once in a great while, however, one will encounter an almost-original, unmodified example, a benchmark aircraft that can be used to refresh faded memories of "the way we were." We found such a Bonanza in serial number D-1052, a straight-35 built in October of 1947 and proudly held in trust by Greg Harrison of Winterset, Iowa. D-1052 had been restored to a near-perfect representation of Walter Beech's competition-gobbling speedster.

The airplane had been updated with an E-185-11 205-hp engine, but the original -1 engine was located in Kansas City and purchased so it could be overhauled and reunited with the airframe in which it left the factory. Meanwhile, the old wooden-blade propeller was found to be no longer airworthy, so a metal-blade Beech controllable pitch propeller was reluctantly fitted and the original propeller was restored to display condition.

Walkaround

We proceeded with an external walk-around of Five-Four-Victor. The Beech propeller is distinguished by a large ring gear behind the spinner for pitch changes. Although no governor was fitted to the Harrison airplane, a constant-speed unit was developed by Beech in later years. As parts for the pitch motors grew increasingly scarce, the prop governors fell from favor as there was little incentive to add wear by continual governing. "I change pitch just three times on each flight," Harrison says, "on the runup, after liftoff and before landing."

The engine can be laid bare with a few twists of a screwdriver in the cam-lock fasteners, allowing the cowling half to be swung up and propped open. The Continental E-series engine is a big, slow-turning six-cylinder mill with sand-cast cooling fins and an external oil supply. The tank is on the left side of the firewall, where oil is picked up by the engine-driven pump, circulated through the engine, and returned for cooling. A radiator built into the tank is fed cooling air from the rear engine baffle. Due to the probability of oil draining back into the engine past the tank's shutoff valve while parked overnight (leading to a false indication of low oil level) it is best to read the oil dipstick immediately after parking, while the oil is still in the tank.

As with all Bonanzas, the engine is bed-mounted to a keel structure that runs from the nose gear to the tailcone, transmitting less vibration than a tubular firewall-anchored mount. Adjustable cowl flaps and removable maintenance access panels are found on the lower cowling.

The amazing Bonanza wing spans less than 33 feet, yet its thick section provides prodigious lift and allows the maingear to be fully enclosed when retracted. A floating-vane switch for the stall warning horn, new technology in 1947, is installed on the aft upper surface of the left wing. Stall strips are located on both leading edges, along with a landing light at mid-span on each side. A cabin air inlet beside the pilot's knee is fed by a small opening in the left wing root; later versions had a copilot's vent as well, with an inlet in the right wing. Harrison says the overhead scoop in the cabin roof is vital to adequately cool the cabin and it retracts to cut drag when not in use. For ventilation while on the ground, the rear windows of the cabin may be propped open about 4 inches.

The classic Beech has electrically-operated landing gear with 6.50 x 8 main tires—Harrison's airplane retained the Goodyear floating-disc brakes. The nose gear uses a 5.00 x 5 tire, folding aft behind doors that leave the rear portion of the wheel-well uncovered. Later versions had longer nose-gear doors to fully cover the opening. Because the nose gear does not steer on the pre-1949 Bonanzas, one keeps the brakes in good working order. Emergency extension utilizes a hand crank.

A 120-pound-capacity baggage compartment behind the rear seats is reached through a door on the right side of the fuselage and opens with the ignition/door key. The boarding step retracts when the nose gear comes up, sliding back into place when the gear is lowered. The aft fuselage once had a trailing-wire low-frequency antenna that could be unreeled through a fairlead on top of the aft cabin. The drogue for the retracted antenna would have been nestled into a holder between the V-stabilizers, attached to the long wire that ran forward to the cabin roof.

Farther aft, the signature V-type tailplanes sit at a 30-degree dihedral angle, changed to 33 degrees with a 20% increase in tailplane chord on the

The Bonanza's famous "butterfly" tail was chosen to reduce drag by eliminating one surface. Only minimal speed was gained by this feature, however.

1951 C35. The dual trim tabs have no camber and do not extend significantly beyond the trailing edge of the ruddervator, both changes that were incorporated later. A plastic stinger on the end of the tailcone once housed a loop antenna for homing with an LF (low frequency) radio.

Bonanza Flying

We were eager to fly the priceless Harrison antique, so a step onto the wingwalk had us heading for the left side of the cockpit. The original Bonanzas did not have individually adjusting seats and the single throwover control yoke was used throughout Bonanza production, although the slim wheel was not. Harrison also had no brakes on his side, so he was certainly hoping we weren't going to let the historic ship get away from us.

The panel's arrangement was chosen for style, not function, but one must remember the simpler times of 1947. A single radio was considered adequate for even IFR work, and a turn needle, slip ball and airspeed indicator were the basics of blind flying. The single fuel gauge had to be switched to display the contents of the tank in use. Not a few pilots have changed tanks without moving the gauge switch, until a surging engine brought them back to reality. The two landing light switches have tactile identification; one dot under the taxi light switch, two under the landing light switch. A single amber or green light shows the landing gear position, backed up by a mechanical indicator in the nosegear well. Likewise, the flaps are signaled up or down by red or green lights.

Not a restoration, this is an original Bonanza panel from 1947, including the radio. Only instrument markings and a newer nav/comm have been added. The slim control wheel on the throwover yoke was used through 1949. No nosegear steering was provided, requiring use of the toe brakes.

The fuel selector under the pilot's left knee incorporated a manual wobble pump in the handle, used to pressurize the carburetor for starting. If the engine-driven pump should fail, this pump would be the only means of keeping the engine going until a landing could be made, so most owners of older Bonanzas installed electric boost pumps to obviate this concern. The left tank should always be selected first when departing with full tanks, as the pressure carburetor returns excess fuel to the left tank, and use of the right tank with a full left one will simply cause fuel to be vented overboard.

NC4854V was reweighed after its restoration and tipped the scales at 1,684 pounds, so a full load of fuel would leave 662 pounds for cabin payload. Two up, we were departing about 300 pounds under gross. We found the switches for the battery and 25-amp generator with the circuit breakers, under a door on the right subpanel. However, Beech also had a "battery" position between "off" and "left/right" on the magneto switch, so one could leave the master switches on all the time and just shut everything down with the key. Wobbling up a bit of boost pressure, we pushed the button to crank the E-185-1 and were rewarded with immediate ignition.

There being little to check (oil pressure up, door latched, etc.), we taxied forth and proceeded to weave across the taxiway like a drunken sailor. We finally got the hang of toe-tapping to steer the Bonanza, and after finding the end of the runway we did a runup at 1,700 rpm to check mags and the electric propeller control, assuring ourselves that it would decease and increase rpm. Harrison seldom opens the cowl flaps, except in extremely hot conditions. A double check is made of door and window security, then we charged off, with a few sashays across the centerline until the rudder circuit came alive.

Normal takeoffs are made flaps up, but if the need arises the use of flaps will get the airplane into the air a full 10 mph sooner. Rotating at about 60 mph, we were off around the 1,000-foot mark. Climbing at 100 mph, approximately the best-rate speed, we immediately reduced rpm to 2,100 before exceeding the one-minute 185 horsepower rating, after which we were limited to 165 hp. The climb-out at 100 mph showed us 900 fpm, even with power reduced to 24 inches m.p.; a more aggressive 78-mph climb yielded 1,200 fpm briefly.

Leveled at 3,500 feet MSL, we idled along reflecting on just how far we've come with light retractables since 1947. The sleek, agile Model 35's greatest advantage over its competition was its ability to retain performance even with power reduced. It could deliver a 150 mph indicated cruise on 9.5 gph at 5,000 feet, according to Greg Harrison, using 20 inches m.p. and 2,050 rpm. We were using only 1,950 rpm and 20 inches m.p. in continuous light chop, but were still indicating 138 mph. This equates to a true airspeed of 150 mph, not bad for an old airplane that wasn't even breathing hard. Pulling 70% power at 10,000 feet, it'll true out at 175 mph, according to the factory specs. We reduced power to 17 inches and saw 120 mph indicated, for a long-range TAS of 131 mph.

Once airborne, the Bonanza could run with the DC-3 airliners of the day, with only 165 maximum-continuous horsepower. The polished skin was standard until 1950, and NC numbers were required on wings and tailcone.

The noise level and cabin room are reasonably good. The seats sit well off the floor for chair-like support and legroom. Shoulder room in the 50-inch-wide cabin is a bit snug, however. The cathedral-like windows give excellent visibility, even in a right turn.

Much has been made of the V-tail Bonanza's tendency to wiggle in rough air, when a dutch-roll coupling of yaw and roll occurs as the airplane "hunts" for smooth air. The oscillations are more a function of the relatively short fuselage than the tail's lack of stabilizing power, but most Bonanza pilots leave their feet on the rudder pedals to dampen the excursions.

Trying to slow down quickly in any Bonanza is an exercise in patience, particularly so in the Straight 35; maximum gear extension speed is 125 mph, and the flaps can only be lowered below 100 mph. After a few minutes at 10 inches m.p., we were down to clean-configuration slowflight. The airplane slow-flew nicely at 60 mph IAS, and a power-off stall with gear and flaps up showed a warning light at 70, then a mild break at 62 mph. With it all hanging out, we got a light at 60 and a buffet and dropoff at 53 mph.

We returned to the field for some landing practice, beginning our entry to the pattern far enough out to reach gear speed on the downwind leg. This reduced speed to 100 mph handily, and a normal pattern could be flown with little power change. Adding partial flaps on base leg at 90 knots, we retrimmed slightly and flew the final with full flaps at 80 mph, hardly a typical high-performance approach speed. Even so, the Bonanza floated for 500 feet or more before touching down; clearly, the early, lightweight Bonanzas can be safely flown at lower approach speeds than their heavyweight descendants.

If you're of a mind to preserve a classic retractable, the high-stepping early Bonanza might be a good choice. Be aware, however, that it is a old complex airplane with many expensive parts that may be needing replacement.

Using similar engines, the Navion cruised about 20 mph slower and lacked the Bonanza's panache, while the wood-and-fabric taildragger Bellanca was viewed as antiquated. All three airplanes eventually became heavier, more powerful and expensive, leaving the light retractable class to be rediscovered by Al Mooney.

5 · The Beechcraft Sierra

After the Bonanza had evolved from a 2,550-pound, 185-hp light re-tractable into a 3,400-pound, 285-hp heavyweight over 20 years, Beech Aircraft discovered a need for a Beechcraft to compete with Mooney and Piper in the category of 180-to-200-hp gear-up fourplacers. To do this, Beech engineers followed the Piper Arrow example by creating a retractable version of the Musketeer, the econo-single that had been developed as Beech's entry-level airplane. Musketeers had a reputation for being rather pedestrian, plain-Jane airplanes, solid and dependable if not fast and flashy.

The Musketeer Super R, as the new retractable was known when it came out in 1970, more or less continued in that vein, attracting little attention after

The Sierra C24R is a comfortable, nice-flying light retractable, with quality features not found in other aircraft. The fourth side window denoted the 200-hp Musketeers.

its debut. Compounding its lackluster market splash was the reluctance of the average Beech dealer to promote anything less than the Bonanza. Accustomed to pursuing potential buyers who met the Bonanza-owner profile, the dealers weren't too aggressive in going down into the under classes of society to sell lower-priced machines.

And so, Beech's new light retractable faced an uphill battle against strong outside competitors like Mooneys and Arrows, as well as internal apathy from the sales force. Small wonder that it never sold strongly, even though it was a basically-sound airplane. Once you've made a conscious decision to accept comfort and durability over raw speed, the Beech Sierra, as it was later called, is a thoroughly acceptable option as a used light retractable.

Baby Beech Pedigree

To understand the Sierra, one must take a look at its pedigree; Beech's light singles began with certification of the foundation Model 23 Musketeer on February 20, 1962. The new baby Beech featured such non-Beechcraft concepts as bonded aluminum honeycomb construction, a stabilator tail and rubber-cushioned gear of trailing-link geometry. The simple 160-hp design lent itself well to high-volume production; unfortunately, Beech was traditionally oriented toward hand-crafted, low-volume, high-quality products, not airplanes that were stamped out and pasted together.

The Musketeer A23 upgrade came in 1963 with a 165-hp fuel-injected Continental engine and in 1966 it was joined by an A23-19 Sport, a 150-hp two-plus-two convertible trainer, along with an A23-24 200-hp Musketeer Super III. The latter airplane, which was subsequently modified into the Super R, was legally entitled to carry up to six people, using a child's seat in the baggage compartment. In 1968, a 180-hp B23 Custom replaced the A23.

Viewed as stepping-stone airplanes leading to eventual Bonanza ownership, the Musketeers had been offered with an optional retractable-gear simulation kit, incorporating a wheel-shaped switch that one could raise after takeoff, extinguishing green gear-down lights even though the wheels remained firmly fixed. A gear-up warning horn would dutifully sound if the throttle was retarded with the ersatz "gear" switch in the up position. The idea was to prepare Musketeer flyers for greater things, of course.

When it became obvious that many of the potential Bonanza buyers were opting for Piper's less-expensive Arrow or the parsimonious Mooney, Beech quickly engineered a real retractable Musketeer, in which the gear switch would do more than activate lights and horns. As with most of the competitors except Mooney, an electrically-powered hydraulic gear system moved the wheels up and down. The rubber-biscuit shock struts were retained, but a smaller 5.00 x 5 nose wheel was used in place of the fat 6.00 x 6 or 15–6.00 x 6 tires

The fixed-gear Beech Musketeer/Sundowner, from which the Sierra was developed.

Seen from below, the Sierra's nose gear has been twisted 90 degrees to stow flat against the fuselage and the main gear is nestled outboard into the faired wheel wells.

on the fixed-gear airplanes. The retractable Musketeer's main wheels swung outward to stow into open wheel wells, avoiding a relocation of the fuel tanks farther away from the center of gravity, which would have created the potential for a wing-heavy imbalance, similar to that of the Piper Cherokee. The nose gear rotated 90 degrees as it folded aft, into a flat stowed position that didn't encroach on engine or cabin space.

Beech's A24R was certificated in both normal and utility category on December 23, 1969. The airplane was dubbed the Super R because it used the 200-hp IO-360 engine and optional constant speed propeller of the Musketeer Super III. The Sierra nametag didn't come along until 1972, when the 180-hp fixed-gear airplane became the Sundowner. One judges the Musketeer line by the window count; two side windows were the hallmark of the 150-hp Sport, three windows denoted the 180-hp Sundowner and the 200-hp airplanes could have a small fourth window if the child's seat were ordered. A left-hand cabin door, to match the standard one on the right, had been developed as an option in 1966 and it was to become standard in 1972.

The B24R Sierra was certificated in June of 1973 in normal category only, with a change to a smaller Hartzell propeller from the A24R's McCauley and a return to conventional round engine instruments; vertical-readout gauges had been briefly offered as an option. Quadrant-style power levers were also introduced. Certificated in October of 1976, the C24R replaced the B24R, with a higher-activity, larger diameter propeller and a general aerodynamic cleanup to boost performance, raising cruise speed by seven mph. The C24R featured under-wing fairings to help streamline the protruding wheels, and the large wing/aileron gap was tightened up. The C24R was produced through 1983, at which time Sierra production was discontinued, due to the general malaise of the industry. In 14 years, Beech built 794 Model 24 retractables, of which 149 were the A24R.

Flight Check

Externally, the Beech Sierra is similar in size to the Bonanza, a bit less than 33 feet in wingspan and a shade over 25 feet in length. The cabin width, benefiting from a visible upper-frame bulge that was developed in 1970 to increase shoulder room over the original box-like Musketeer, is actually wider than a Bonanza's. The Musketeer series always presented a lofty, coltish look on the ground, due to the tall landing gear without wheel pants. The Sierra's open-

The Sierra C24R, the last model produced, was distinguished by streamlining fairings aft of the main gear wheel well. With its smaller nose wheel and prominent gear doors, the Sierra is definitely not a Sundowner.

framework retractable gear is similar in appearance, particularly because the gear leg's door is on the inboard side, leaving the strut visible to passersby.

The glass-cloth and epoxy-resin cowling is secured by quick-release fasteners and does not open for preflight inspection, save for an oil-check door atop the engine. No cowl flaps are fitted to the IO-360, and a polished spinner sets off the airplane's lines. Fresh-air intakes at the base of the windshield feed eyeball vents in the panel and an inlet on the tail's dorsal fin pressurizes the overhead vents. Exhaust air exits through a grill above the hat shelf, with an outlet on the left rear side of the fuselage.

The laminar-flow NACA 63_2 A415 wing offers only 146 square feet of area. Thus, relatively long-span slotted flaps of 35° extension are needed to meet the statutory 61-knot maximum stall speed in landing configuration. No stall strips are used to artificially induce stall indications. The external hinging of the flaps contributes to the Sierra's parasite drag. Both electric and manual flaps were offered, although the majority of Sierras were equipped with the electrically-driven system.

The Sierra's ailerons are interconnected to the rudder by a bungee spring to enhance stability, and the rudder pedals are linked to the nose gear with stiff steering springs, so one meets with a certain amount of resistance when wiggling the controls during preflight. Each wingtip carries a landing light, with an extra taxi light provided on the left side.

The fuel system consists of integral fuel bays of nearly 60-gallons capacity (59.8, to be exact). Usable fuel varies from 58.8 gallons in the A24R to 52 gallons in the B24R and back up to 57.2 gallons in the C24R. The floor-mounted fuel selector, protected by a dog-dish cup to ward off errant kicks,

The Sierra main gear retracts outboard to avoid relocating the integral fuel tank bays. This B24 has no after-body fairing.

has no "Both On" position, but there are two "Off" selections, reached by depressing a retrofitted lockout spring. Tabs in the filler openings allow fueling to 15- or 20-gallon levels, as one doesn't normally require six hours of cruise endurance. Fuel in excess of 20 gallons is not gaugeable.

The landing gear is powered by an electrically-driven hydraulic power-pack in the aft fuselage. Emergency extension is a simple matter of dumping hydraulic pressure with a special twist-tool and allowing the gear to free-fall into position. The prominent springs in the main gear's linkage provide extra overcenter inertia for extension. Because of the limited travel of the rubber-cushioned gear legs, the Sierra uses an airspeed sensor to disable the hydraulic powerpack on the ground, rather than a squat switch; approximately 60 knots are needed to close the safety switch.

An optional safety landing gear system was offered, automatically extending the gear below 100 knots if power is reduced and preventing retraction if the throttle position doesn't approximate 18 inches MP. An on/off switch allowed the pilot to disable the safety system if required.

The overly-large baggage door on the left side of the fuselage is equipped with an inside latch release, as it is used to enter and leave the optional child's

Originally developed for the Musketeer Super, the Sierra's large baggage door allows access to the optional child's seat.

As with Cessna's Cardinals, Beech only used a stabilator tail on the Musketeer series.

seat, a miniature two-place version of the regular seats. A typical installation of this seat restricts the 270-pound baggage allowance to 203 pounds.

The 12-volt battery is installed in the tail cone, and a center-pin type auxiliary power plug is located on the right rear fuselage. At serial number MC-647, midyear 1979, Beech switched the Sierras to a 28-volt system, with either one 24-volt or two 12-volt batteries provided.

The Sierra's tail uses Beech's only foray into stabilators. The stabilator allows the Musketeer to have a wider CG range. An anti-servo trim tab balances the slab tail's movements. The rudder is devoid of either trim tabs or bungee trim adjustment.

Making an Entrance

Boarding the Sierra is a pleasure, with the twin doors allowing the occupants to enter from either wingwalk. The rear seats are reached by a simple step down into the cabin, while the front seats require a slight hip-swivel. The wing spar runs under the rear passengers' knees, but legroom is not inhibited. Tubular braces at the corner of the windshields, a Model 23 trademark, provide a finger hold for front-seat adjustment. Closing the Sierra doors is a joy, compared with those of other low-wing airplanes; just slam them shut and

With the added left entrance door, the Sierra and Commander 112 are the only low-wing light retractables offering simultaneous boarding.

forget them. There are no extra latches to engage, no need to verify that hooks are caught. Evidently the slightly smaller size of the Beech doors avoids some of the suck-open problems of low-wing hatches.

Outfitted with a typical radio package, a specimen Sierra we tested weighed 1,845 pounds, leaving a scant 523 pounds available for cabin payload after the tanks were topped off. However, four 170-pound people could be carried with 37.5 gallons of fuel, enough for a three-hour mission. As a

The Sierra C24R instrument panel reflected Beechcraft quality and workmanship; brace tubes in windshield and straight-up center console are trademarks of the series.

six-placer, a reasonable load would be two 170-pound men, two 115-pound women and two children of 50 pounds each, allowing nearly 40 gallons to be carried.

Starting follows a modified Lycoming fuel-injection sequence; throttle cracked, mixture rich, boost pump on for three seconds, then off. Hot starts are performed with the mixture in idle cutoff, advanced to rich as the engine starts. A starter-engaged warning light was installed in Sierras from 1981 on, signaling a stuck starter relay. Once the engine is running, the radio master switch is flicked on and the throttle pushed up to move out of the chocks. Taxiing is straightforward, with some hobbyhorse rocking on uneven surfaces, typical of the stiff, short-wheelbase gear.

Ready For Takeoff

Pre-takeoff checks include a magneto check and propeller exercise at 2,000 rpm and a check of the electric trim movement by observing the manual trim wheel's actions. Flaps are set to 15° for takeoff and, unlike other Lycoming-powered light retractables, the boost pump stays off for takeoff. Acceleration at light weights is good, although the Beech airplanes were never noted for being strong short-field performers. Rotation at 60 to 65 knots transitions into a liftoff at 70 or so, using about 1,200 feet of runway. I prefer to see 80 to 85 knots before retracting the flaps, usually reached just about the time the runway disappears and the gear is brought up. A slight yawing motion is felt as the nose gear twists into its well.

Best rate-of-climb speed is 85 knots, which can produce 1,000 fpm at light weights, although 700 to 800 fpm is more typical. V_X is 71 knots, and the cruise climb of 96 knots provides a comfortable deck angle. When leveling out into cruise, there is little to do other than tweak the mixture.

At 3,500 feet, we turned the test airplane to 25-square power briefly, about 80% power, and trued out at 130 knots on a fuel burn of just over 12 gph. A more-typical power setting of 24 inches m.p. and 2400 rpm, roughly 70% power on a tad over 10 gph, gave us a TAS of 127 knots. A 65% power setting of 22 inches and 2,400 rpm gave us a true airspeed of 121 knots, on about 8.5 gph and a 55% long-range power setting at 20 inches and 2400 rpm gave a 115-knot TAS.

The visibility at cruise is not as superb as it is in the Bonanza, but it is still good; the Sierra pilot sits on the wing's leading edge, allowing nearly straight-down visibility to the side, and the extensive windows allow one to scan the horizon from tail tip to tail tip. Only overhead, above the window line, is a blind spot apparent.

Control feel is nicely harmonized; the ailerons are powerful and smooth. Unfortunately, the barrel and aileron rolls allowed in the special aerobatic versions of the fixed-gear airplanes were never approved for the Sierras, and even the utility category A24R was not approved for spins.

A nice flying, nice looking, quality-built airplane, the Beech Sierra is a standout in-flight or on the ramp. The large baggage door, seen here at the left rear of the cabin, allowed the installation of a child's seat in the baggage area.

Slowed down, we found the Sierra nicely controllable at 70 knots. In power-off stalls, we encountered a full break at 62 knots IAS with flaps and gear up, decreasing to 52 knots when we extended flaps and gear. No untoward tendencies were noted in stalls, which required perhaps 300 feet for recovery. The landing gear is placarded against retraction above 113 knots, although it can be extended at speeds up to 135 knots. Flaps are prohibited above 96 knots.

Returning for landings, we dropped the gear on downwind, using 80 knots for maneuvering in the pattern with half flaps, slowing to 75 knots on final and 70 or so over the fence. The Sierra lands easily and predictably, although it is important to use firm back pressure to hold the nose up at forward CG loadings. The 12-foot-wide main gear stance and trailing arm suspension forgives most bobbles, although smooth landings are elusive. For maximum braking, it is necessary to raise the flaps after touchdown. Otherwise, the main tires may slide because of the wheelbarrowing effect of the flaps. It is possible to land much shorter than one can take off; I routinely stopped in 1,000 feet of runway.

The Sierra is a comfortable, dependable cruiser, giving 140-mph performance in a large cabin with durable fittings. There are few airframe-related airworthiness directives on the machine, limited to flap and trim tab linkages and the aforementioned fuel selector guard. The airframe is sturdy, although one might watch for protruding wing skins above the main gear attachments, a sign of hard landings in the aircraft's history.

If your search for the perfect light retractable leads to Beechcraft quality and a relatively large cabin, you'll enjoy the Sierra's mild manners. It's well worth serious consideration. If you prefer your wing to be positioned above the cabin, however, you'll no doubt want to take a look at the Cessna light retractables, as reviewed in the next chapters.

6 · Cessna's First Light Retractable
The Cardinal RG

As Cessna undertook to redesign its light single-engine airplanes in the late 1960s, in an attempt to update its series of strut-braced high-wingers, a totally-new design called the Cardinal emerged as Cessna's "plane of the 70s." This new basic airplane of the Cessna line was intended to retain all of the old Skyhawk's attributes and overcome many of its disadvantages.

The high wing was sacrosanct, of course ("ever see a low-winged bird?" was a favorite Cessna ad quip), but the struts weren't, so the Cardinal's wing was cantilevered from a hefty carry-through member atop the cabin. The Skyhawk's big cabin doors, on both sides of the cabin, were indispensable, but they were widened and the fuselage lowered to eliminate the awkward load-

Even with the wheels fixed down, the Cessna Cardinal was an attractive design.

ing shuffle of the 'Hawk. No-maintenance spring steel main gear struts were another favorite feature of the Skyhawk; but the Cardinal went the 'Hawk's flat struts one better with *tubular* struts that could absorb shock in all directions. And to assure that the roomy Cardinal cabin could be loaded with little regard to C.G. constraints, Cessna's first-ever stabilator tail was fitted.

All the hype and hoopla was for naught; customers preferred the familiar old 172 over the new 177 Cardinal. Cessna was forced to redefine the Cardinal's market toward a narrower, more upscale niche. Despite some minor teething troubles in its infancy, the Cardinal acquired an aura of exclusivity, offering looks, comfort and distinction to separate its owners from the masses of Skyhawkers. About this same time, Cessna was rapidly expanding its line of airplanes to cover any marketing opportunity, from trainers to agplanes to jets, so there was an obvious need for a 200-hp retractable-gear ship to compete with the Mooneys and Arrows. What better candidate for this task than Cessna's great hope of the future gone sour, the Cardinal?

Thus, Cessna engineers were given the task of folding the Cardinal's wheels away, to fit into a gear-up niche below the Centurion. While the limited space made this a challenge, experience with the 210's highly-articulated legs made it doable. As the cycle of retraction began, the main gear drooped downward to reduce its span to the width of the fuselage, then the legs swung up and aft to slip into open slots and wells under the belly. The slim tubular gear legs took up little room, but the wheels and tires required a hump in the baggage compartment. Meanwhile, the nose-gear tire and oleo strut slipped aft into the lower engine compartment. The only gear doors used were small flaps to cover the nose gear; the rest of the gear was left exposed for simplicity.

Naturally, the system was hydraulically operated, given Cessna's long association with fluid power that had grown into a large separate division serving non-aviation markets. However, the Cardinal used an electrically-driven powerpack producing 1,500 p.s.i., rather than an engine-driven pump. The Cardinal RG's four-cylinder Lycoming was a fuel-injected 200-hp IO-360 instead of the 180-hp carbureted O-360 of the fixed-gear Cardinal. The main tires were downsized to low-profile 15 x 6.00–6s to gain a bit more clearance in the wheel wells, while a standard 5.00–5 nose tire was used. Initially, the RG used white-sidewall tires, for an extra touch of class.

Other than the engine upgrade and the landing gear system, the Cardinal RG shared the same production line features as the fixed gear Cardinal. The first Cardinal RG was marketed as a 1971 model, having achieved certification on August 11, 1970, roughly 3 years after its fixed-gear sibling. By then, the standard Cardinal had grown to 2,500 pounds; the RG tipped the scales at 2,800 pounds. The four-place cabin was the same for both aircraft, other than for a telescoping manual hydraulic pump in the floor between the front seats and a slight hump in the floor in the aft cabin for the gear system.

The Cardinals were produced through 1978, when Cessna finally threw in the towel and gave up on its 10-year-long battle to find the airplane's niche.

This 1971 Cardinal RG was part of the first year's production. Steady improvements followed through the 8-year life of the design.

The fixed-gear Cardinal was never able to find acceptance, either as a Sky-hawk replacement or on its own, and its cost of production made it unrealistically expensive for a step-up airplane. Shutting down the Cardinal line meant the end of RG production as well, even though the retractable outsold the fixed-gear machine over the total 8-year lifespan. Some 1,314 Cardinal RGs were built, plus another 176 Reims Cardinal RGs that were built in the Reims, France facility.

Sought after as an efficient, comfortable light retractable right up to the end of its production run, the Cardinal RG continues to be a readily salable commodity on the used market. The airplanes were steadily improved over the years, so, all things being equal, the later models become progressively more desirable. An improved propeller boosted cruise speed by five mph in 1972, larger fuel tanks were fitted in 1973, a simpler gear system was introduced in 1974, the baggage compartment was enlarged in 1975, and an improved instrument panel came along in 1976. See the chronology listing on page 130 for details.

Subject Airplanes

As with most of the chapters in this book, we flew more than one Cardinal RG to research the type, from a 1971 version to a 1977 model. N8219G was a basic 1971 first-year example; it had accumulated 3,200 hours at the time of our visit, having had its engine majored at the 2,000-hour point. The

The Cardinal RG's nose gear is mounted farther forward, retracting aft into the lower engine compartment while the main gear swings inboard and aft. Both fixed-gear and retractable Cardinals have cowl flaps, but only the 1971 Cardinal RG had fixed boarding steps. A sleek cowling with landing lights was introduced in 1973.

owner felt the RG offered the best mix of features for commuting among his dispersed family. He flew it from a 2,200-foot grass runway beside his ranch home, which was quite ample at an elevation of 1,300 feet.

A preflight walkaround revealed a few of the unique Cardinal features not shared by the rest of the Cessna line. The engine compartment is compact, more like a Mooney's engine room than the spacious Skyhawk cowling, which had begun life housing a six-cylinder powerplant. As with most Cessnas, the pilot can only guess about the health of the appliances under the cowling; an oil access door is the sole opening unless one wishes to attack the quick-release fasteners with a screwdriver. Induction air is taken through an air filter inside the left cowl opening, while a NACA ramp on the right side of the cowling feeds an oil cooler. Small adjustable cowl flaps are fitted to the lower lip of the cowling, and the large single exhaust tailpipe is curved aft, rather than jutting straight down as with the fixed gear Cardinal. A squat switch on the nose-gear strut inhibits the gear system's electric powerpack while on the ground.

The first two years of Cardinal RG production offered a blunt cowling nose cap with moldings that give a rather mustachioed look to the aircraft; a sleeker cowling was introduced in 1973, when the landing lights were moved from the left wingtip to the nose cap.

The Cardinal RG's full-cantilever wing, similar to that of the 1967 and later Centurions, features wide-span electrically-operated flaps, adjustable to any desired degree of deflection up to the full 30 degrees. The ailerons are Frise-type paddles, incorporating an interconnect linkage with the rudder to aid coordination and dampen adverse yaw. Fuel vent tubes project aft just outboard of the ailerons; check valves notwithstanding, parking on a slope invites siphoning fuel overboard if tanks are full. Wing dihedral is a nominal 1.5 degrees.

The fuel system consists of two wet-wing fuel bays; the 1971 and 1972 models had a 51 gallon capacity, with 61 gallon tanks standard from 1973 on. Markers in the large tanks' filler necks allow fueling to 22 gallons each. Small reservoir tanks are used to assure a positive flow of fuel, and the boost pump is only required for starting and backup, not takeoff and landing. The early Cardinal RG had a fuel selector with just on and off positions, but a four-way selector was introduced in 1973. Cardinals were also originally equipped with flush-fitting filler caps whose fold-down handles were noted for admitting water when sitting out in the rain. Most Cessnas have had the leak-resistant umbrella caps retrofitted, a wise move.

A 120-pound capacity baggage compartment behind the rear seats is divided into two loading areas by the massive wheel well growing into its volume. The compartment was expanded aft approximately 12 inches, compared with the fixed gear Cardinal. A small shelf protruding into the tailcone was added in 1975, accommodating up to 12 pounds of light objects. The door is a truncated rectangle to accommodate the wheel well opening, hinging upward with a spring-loaded arm to keep it off one's noggin. Like the upper cowling, it is of bonded construction, rather than a riveted assembly. Both the hydraulic powerpack for the landing gear and the battery are located in the tailcone behind the baggage compartment wall.

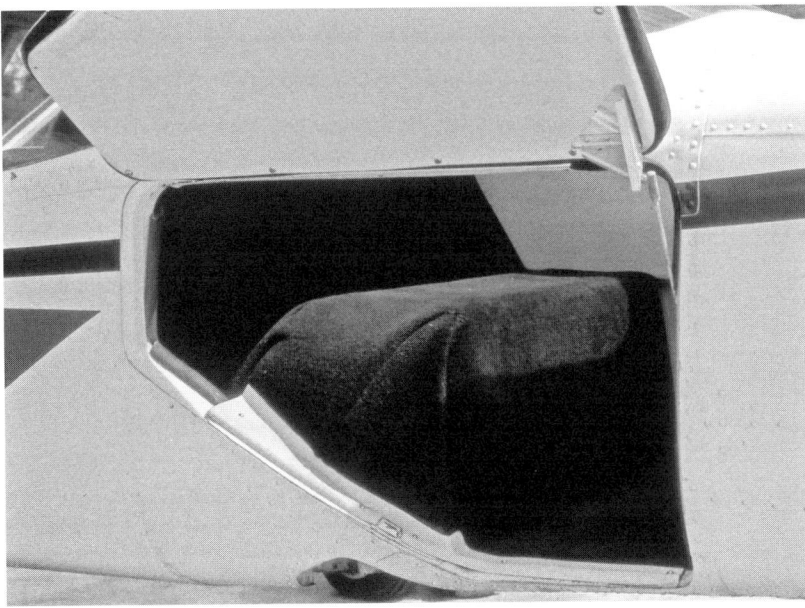

The "permanent suitcase" in the Cardinal RG's baggage compartment is the main gear wheel well fixture. Ample room remains fore and aft of the obstruction, however.

The Cardinal RG inherited the slotted stabilator used on the fixed-gear Cardinal; it was Cessna's only use of an all-flying tail.

The rudder tip is 8 feet, 7 inches above ramp level, and the rudder can be trimmed for long climbs or yaw corrections by an adjustable bungee in the circuit. Cessna's one-and-only attempt at using a stabilator tail spans nearly 12 feet, balanced by an anti-servo tab to provide good control. The stabilator is slotted to ward off airflow separation at high angles of attack. It's a good idea to peek into the stinger's slot for signs of bird nests; the little feathered friends like to pack the tip of the tailcone full, which can interfere with control travel. The rather thin leading edge skins of the stabilator can be easily damaged by stones thrown up by the main gear and propeller, so gravel abrasion boots are a must if one operates from such surfaces, and even then dents are inevitable.

Step Right Up

Boarding is a quick, direct process, thanks to the big doors, but one has to hang on to them to avoid broken stops and hinges if they are opened with a following wind. Boarding steps hanging down from the lower fuselage are the hallmark of the 1971 RG; these were removed on the 1972 model in favor of step pads on the gear legs. As with the other Cessnas, loading the front seats first and sliding them forward into flying position increases room for the rear passengers. Our test airplane's pilot seat was fitted with an add-on auxiliary seat latch, in case the primary latch slips; as with the fuel cap change, it's a good idea. Once everyone is inside, the door's handle is rotated forward to snug the door tightly shut. Should a door pop open in flight it may be reclosed without difficulty. Triangular crank-open wind wings in the door windows

The massive Cardinal RG doors must be opened with care when parking with a tailwind. Boarding access couldn't be easier.

are an effective source of ground ventilation after the engine starts; maximum speed for opening them in flight is 105 knots.

Among the chief attractions of the Cardinal series is its low floor level, allowing front seat passengers of average height to simply slide into their seat from the ground. Rear passengers require a bit more clambering, but they still have an easier time of it than in most airplanes. Usable room, on the other hand, is compromised by the low ceiling height; the rear seats sit quite low, and even with this compromise adults will find their heads brushing the ceiling. Up front, the sloping windshield posts seem to block side vision no matter how the seats are adjusted, if one is to reach the rudder pedals. Elbow room and leg room are more than adequate, however, and the cabin measures a generous 42.5 inches wide.

The cockpit floor is relatively unobstructed, other than for the hydraulic hand pump's cover (40 strokes are required to extend the gear if the electric powerpack fails). The fuel valve is on the floor, along with a remote handle for a reservoir tank sump drain under the pilot's seat. Other frequently-used items are on the central pedestal; trim wheels, cowl flap control, microphone, cigar lighter and ash tray. Electrical switches, landing gear switch, power knobs and

Equipped with every imaginable avionics tool, this 1975 Cardinal RG featured the final year of the original "humpback" Cardinal instrument panel.

the infinitely-adjustable wing flap control are found on the subpanel. There is even room for a glove compartment on the extreme right side of the stylish panel; a rearview mirror on top of the panel, comprising more form than function, was a popular option. The distinctive Cardinal humped panel was replaced in 1976 by a more straightforward design.

One-Niner-Golf was fully equipped, although not overly so. An electrically-driven standby vacuum pump was installed, just aft of the firewall, complete with a low-vacuum warning light on the panel. Basic avionics remained Cessna/ARC 300-series units; dual RT-328T navcomm radios, one with glideslope, a CC-310A transponder with an ACK encoder, and an ADF and audio panel.

Thus burdened, the 1971 Cardinal RG weighed in at 1,772 pounds; a full fuel load of 50 usable gallons would still leave 728 pounds for cabin payload, enough for the four standard 170 persons and 48 pounds of baggage. Later versions, of course, have 60 gallons of fuel, which reduces full-fuel payload by 60 pounds. The 1975 model we tested, by comparison, had all the Garmin avionics it could hold, including an MX-20 multifunction display along with the GNS-530 and GNS-430 GPS/Comm/VOR-LOC units, plus a two-axis S-Tec autopilot. It weighed 1,831 pounds empty, leaving 609 pounds for payload after topping the tanks. Thanks to the powerful stabilator, C.G. range is generous, making loading relatively simple as long as one keeps anvils out of the baggage compartment.

For 1976, Cessna Cardinal panels were extended to the right to provide additional room for avionics. This airplane was outfitted with Cessna/ARC radios in the popular Nav-Pac package, supplemented by a Loran unit that's now passé.

Starting cold requires running the boost pump with mixture rich until 4 gph of fuel flow are indicated, then pulling the mixture back to idle cut-off to crank the engine. For a hot start, one leaves the mixture lean and advances the throttle to half-open, cranking without the boost pump. In either case, the engine fires after a few cranks and there is plenty to time to bring the mixture to full-rich.

A touch of throttle moved us easily across the grass, the light nose-gear steering and toe brakes providing precise control. At runway end, we advanced the throttle to 1,800 rpm for magneto and propeller check (there is a yellow caution arc on the tachometer from 1,400 to 1,750 rpm). We switched the boost pump on briefly to check its operation then turned it off, and we confirmed that the cowl flaps were open and the wing flaps set to 10 degrees for takeoff (which serves to shorten the takeoff roll by 15%).

We brought the power up to full bore and accelerated down the turf strip, breaking ground at approximately 60 mph in some 1,000 feet of runway. As soon as a positive climb was observed, ensuring that the drooping main gear would not contact the surface, we flipped the gear switch to up and observed a noticeable trim change as the wheels swung aft. The cycle time is about 12 seconds, except for the fast-acting 28-volt 1978 models. Flaps were raised as we reached 80 mph (airspeed indications were in mph until 1976) and we climbed out at the V_Y of 94 mph, observing a full-bore rate of climb of

This 1975 Cardinal RG has a paint design from a 1997 Skylane. All Cardinal RGs present a similar profile; only the details change over the years.

about 900 fpm. We were loaded to roughly 350 pounds under gross, but the temperature was in the high 90s.

A top-of-the-green power setting of 25 inches and 2,500 rpm gave us an 800 fpm rate of climb, and with the nose lowered to achieve a 500-fpm rate of climb the airspeed increased to 110 mph. We leveled out at 4,500 feet to do some cruise and handling checks. At 24 inches m.p. and 2,500 rpm, about 75% power, we were indicating a solid 155 mph for a TAS of 171 mph (149 knots) on a fuel burn of 11 gph. Under similar conditions on its test flight, the cleaner 1975 model moved into the yellow arc at 160 mph to indicate 170, a TAS of 182 mph (158 knots). For economy cruising, we tuned the 1971 airplane to 21 inches m.p. and 2,200 rpm, just under 55% power, which resulted in an IAS of 130 mph on a Skyhawk's fuel burn of 8.5 gph, a true airspeed of 143 mph (124 knots). Whatever the model year, the Cardinal RG can provide fast, economical transportation with a comfortable cabin.

Handling is delightful; the airplane is stable when trimmed up for cruise, yet is responsive when the controls are thrown around, particularly the silky-smooth ailerons. The interconnect is not noticeable, yet it evidently produces well-coordinated turns without concentrating on rudder application. Slowed down to check low-speed handling, the Cardinal RG flew around comfortably at 70 mph with flaps up. Power off, the clean configuration resulted in a stall warning at 73 mph, followed by a clean break at 68 mph. Flaps and gear

Seen in-flight, the strutless Cardinal RG is as sleek as its low-wing competition. It offers an unmatched view of the landscape, has a comfortable cabin and excellent cross-country performance.

down, the warning began at 63 mph and we ran out of stabilator at 55 mph without ever inducing a stall break. The first 10 degrees of flap can go out at 150 mph, the landing gear can be extended at 140 mph or less and full flaps are allowed below 110 mph. Unlike the dual-category fixed-gear Cardinal, the 177RG is strictly a normal category airplane, with no spins allowed.

Cleaned up for our descent to the traffic pattern, we swung the gear down once more on the downwind leg, adding enough drag for an easy approach at 80 mph. We lowered 20 degrees of flap on base and went to the 30 degree setting on final, crossing the numbers to close throttle and settle on without difficulty. The Cardinal is unlike the normal elevator-equipped Cessna in its landing characteristics, although it is not difficult to land after one grows accustomed to the stabilator's power. The secret is to never move the stick forward, only aft, in small increments, pausing to allow airspeed to dissipate. Pumping the yoke fore and aft invites a damaging porpoise. Runway length consumed on pavement was about 1,500 feet, with normal braking. Back at the ranch, we stopped in just over half of the 2,200 foot strip, thanks to the drag of the sod.

As an economy retractable, the Cardinal RG is roomy, fast and fun to fly. It handles distinctly unlike the other Cessnas, but has no true bad habits. Maintenance requires the consultation of a knowledgeable Cardinal shop; the nose-gear strut, for instance, is upside down from other Cessna installations.

The AD list primarily concerns engine and auxiliary equipment items, and should be checked along with service bulletins as part of any pre-purchase inspection.

Thankfully, most Cardinal RGs have had the original Cessna ARC radios exchanged for newer gear, although the factory avionics served well in their day. Airframe-wise, buy the latest model you can afford, because they just kept getting better. For a rare combination of load-carrying, comfort and economy, a good Cardinal RG is hard to beat. Now, just try to find an owner who'll part with one.

7 · Cessna's Cutlass RG
The Gentle Retractable

In the world of light retractable-gear airplanes, it might seem uncharacteristic to find an airplane capable of floating across the fence for a landing at 60 knots, or stalling completely power-off at or near the 40-knot mark on the airspeed indicator. Racehorse singles that burn up the skies at 135 knots or more are not usually noted for flying slow and handling like a trainer.

Cessna's Cutlass RG, thanks to its basic Skyhawk roots, probably wins the title of "tamest high-performance airplane." Officially known as the 172RG, the airframe is derived from the tried-and-true model 172 (billed as the World's Most Popular Airplane, with all that entails), inheriting its benign flying traits. Introduced in mid-1979 as a 1980 model, the Cutlass RG was a reasonably straightforward assemblage of off-the-shelf parts; the engine chosen was Lycoming's bulletproof 180-hp O-360, which Cessna had already employed for ten years in the fixed-gear Cardinal, and the landing gear system was very similar to the one used in the Skylane RG, in production since 1978. Even the 66-gallon integral wet-wing fuel tanks had been offered on the 1979 Hawk XP. There were a few ADs (airworthiness directives) issued on the new airplane; the propeller needed dye-checking, the rudder trim bungee required replacement, and some re-work was required in the control system. Once through the shakedown period, however, the Cutlass RG became a relatively trouble-free performer.

Its introduction was stimulated by the gap left in Cessna's product line when Cardinal production ended after 1978. The Cardinal RG had been Cessna's light-retractable standard bearer for eight years, but the low-slung, stabilator-equipped, cantilever-wing Cardinals just never quite fit in with the rest of the line. Having had nothing smaller than a Skylane RG to offer as a gear-up airplane in the 1979 model year, Cessna quickly undertook to convert the Skyhawk to retractable gear.

By upping horsepower from 160 to 180, adding a constant-speed propeller, and swinging the landing gear up out of the slipstream, the Cutlass RG enjoyed a 20-knot speed advantage over the Skyhawk. While capable of 140 knots in brochure quotations, a solid 135 knots was more typically seen. Gross weight of the 172RG was set at 2,650 pounds, versus 2,300 pounds for the

In the air, the tucked-away landing gear makes the Cutlass RG a clean, attractive airplane.

1980 Skyhawk. The entire package was nicely balanced to fit into the niche under the Skylane RG, with four gph less fuel burn and about $17,000 lower base price. By sticking with the carburetor-equipped O-360, rather than the 200-hp fuel-injected IO-360 used by most of the competition, the Cutlass RG enjoyed an inherent price advantage of several thousand dollars.

It was unfortunate that the Cutlass RG appeared just as the great general aviation depression was beginning; only 1,159 were built during the six years of its production, ending with the 1985 models. The base price rose from $48,900 in 1980 to $76,850 in 1985, a whopping 57% increase in only six years. Nevertheless, had the market not collapsed, the Cutlass RG would probably have been built at rates of several hundred per year, most likely with a 200-hp Lycoming option in due time.

Year By Year

Changes in the design were minimal over its production lifespan. The 1981 Cessnas, including the Cutlass RG, incorporated a raucous avionics cooling fan that moved four cubic feet of cooling air per minute through the nav-comms. The fan was hot-wired to the battery switch, rather than the avionics master, and at taxi power it made more noise than the engine. At least there was little excuse for leaving the master switch on after shutting down. Base price was moved up to $52,400.

For 1982, the landing lights were moved from the lower cowling to the left wing's leading edge, where they had been located on Cessnas of a decade earlier. The wing location lessened the impact of vibrations on the lamps and eliminated the need to disconnect the lights' wiring when uncowling the engine. A new three-switch circuit assured that all three landing gear legs would have to be retracted before the amber "gear up" light would illuminate. More ventilation airflow, improved door sealing, and a twist-lock on the glove box door were cockpit improvements. The separate glideslope antenna in the windshield was eliminated in favor of a coupler. A new simplified linkage between the fuel selector and fuel valve was incorporated. Base price was $59,350.

The 1983 models received a new non-shock-mounted instrument panel, a low-vacuum warning light and a quieter avionics cooling fan operating at 50% of the previous fan speed. A heftier control wheel, similar to the Skylane's, was used. The distracting full-time "gear up" light was finally eliminated in favor of a red momentary "unsafe" light that indicated operation of the hydraulic pump motor. This was also the year the FAA reneged on its 1979 approval of three-inch registration numbers for low-speed aircraft, mandating a return to the 12-inch "billboard" numbers on the side of the fuselage for all new airplanes. A bit of confusion entered the Cessna line following the introduction of a fixed-gear Cutlass without the "RG," essentially a 180-hp Skyhawk for high-and-hot operations. Base price was up to $68,300.

In 1984, flush-fitting "popout" camlock cowl fasteners, similar to those used on the larger Cessna singles, replaced the round-head quarter-turn fasteners used previously. Rear seat shoulder harness and dual controls became standard, rather than optional. Base price was $73,900.

The final full year of Cessna's piston-airplane production, 1985, saw the long-established "II" and "NavPac" option packages replaced by "A" and "B" packages, and a new paint design featuring a top cowling painted in trim color, rather than white. The purchase of an optional standby vacuum pump was required if the aircraft was to be certified for IFR. Base price was $76,850.

Many of the Cutlass RGs found their way onto rental and flight training flight lines, due to the ease with which Skyhawk pilots could be turned into official FAA-designated complex airplane pilots. The 172RG neatly filled the requirement for a complex airplane in the curriculum for the commercial pilot rating, and it also made a good instrument trainer, as long as the factory-supplied Cessna/ARC avionics kept working.

Of course some Cutlass RGs were bought by owner/pilots who used them for business and pleasure transportation, rather than as rental ships or trainers. It proved to be an excellent IFR platform and a comfortable traveling machine for owner-flown journeys.

External Inspection

A walkaround shows the salient, Skyhawk-based features, plus some interesting points common only to the 172RG. Indeed, little of the Skyhawk parentage is evident from the firewall forward. There is a larger spinner to cov-

er the hub of the constant-speed propeller, a deeper, more-rounded cowling profile to include the nose-gear wheel-well, and a pair of gapping nose-gear doors that remain open at all times when the gear is down. While no doubt a high-drag item, the fixed gear doors help keep the rigging simple. Two rocket-launcher openings on each side of the gear doors house the landing and taxi lights, inset without benefit of streamlining lenses.

The gear system is hydraulically-actuated, operated by an electrically-driven power pack behind the center console. Unlike the Cardinal RG, the Cutlass RG nose gear folds forward, the doors closing behind it to smooth up the airflow. The main gear, on the other hand, folds inward, then up and aft to stow into open wheel and strut wells under the aft belly. The gear is held up by trapped hydraulic pressure, so emergency extension procedures begin with moving the gear knob to "down" then extending a telescoping hand pump from the floorboards and wobbling it back and forth to expand the gear into the "down and locked" position. A descending paint trim stripe helps camouflage the open main gear wells that notch into the fuselage sides. Small-diameter 15-6.00 x 6 tires are used on the main wheels as with the Cardinal RG, Skylane RG and early 210. A conventional 5.00 x 5 nose tire is fitted.

The Lycoming O-360-F1A6 is buttoned up tightly, with only an oil access door available for preflighting unless one happens to have a screwdriver to unlock the cowling fasteners. A rearward-curving exhaust stack juts below the right side of the cowling, a notch in the right cowl flap being necessary to close around the tailpipe. The factory-supplied, one-size-fits-all, towbar is too short to allow easy ground handling of the Cutlass RG, which has a slightly longer nose than a 172, so some owners have built a longer, custom-made one.

Located in the tailcone for balance (rather than on the firewall), the small 24-volt, 12-cell battery provides more than ample cranking power but costs a pretty penny at replacement time and has a shorter lifespan than a 12-volt battery. The 28-volt system also precludes emergency jump starts from an automobile. On the rare chance that 24-volt ground power will be available when needed, an auxiliary power plug is located in a safe-to-use position on the left side of the aft fuselage.

The classic strut-braced Cessna wing, circa 1949, is retained for the Cutlass RG, with the drooped leading edge added in 1973. The benefits of lighter structure made possible by the single lift strut outweigh the drag resulting from its presence, and it also makes a convenient hand-hold with which to drag the airplane in and out of the hangar. The fundamental airfoil is a relatively high-lift NACA 2412 section, with a constant-chord planform out to the strut fittings and a double-tapered layout from the struts to the tip. Dihedral is a modest 1.5 degrees, due to the inherent stability of hanging the cabin beneath the wing. No stall strips are needed to give aerodynamic indications of

Cowl flaps and smaller main gear tires denote the Cutlass RG, which shares most of the Skyhawk features. The descending paint stripe aft of the cabin hides a notch in the fuselage for the main gear wheel-wells.

the stall. An electrical stall warning vane is on the left wing's leading edge, in place of the pneumatic kazoo of the Skyhawk. Openings in the leading edge near the wing root feed overhead ventilation outlets in the cabin; the inboard openings are for the rear seat vents, the outboard ones are for the pull-out vents in the corners of the windshield.

The flaps are Cessna's massive semi-Fowler slotted surfaces with hidden tracks, electrically extended by a motor in the right wing. Any desired degree of extension can be pre-selected by the lever on the panel, up to the 30-degree maximum; earlier Cessnas had 40-degrees of flap available, but the Cutlass evidently has sufficient drag without the last ten degrees and a full-dirty go-around is easier with less flap. With the reduced maximum flap setting, there is no cautionary placard regarding slips with flaps extended, as there is in the 'Hawk.

The fuel system uses a sealed portion of the wing itself to carry as much as 33 gallons on each side. This gives 62 gallons of usable fuel, a somewhat extravagant amount for a 10 gph engine, so standpipes are provided in the fuel filler necks to allow fueling to a 44-gallon reduced fuel load by filling the tanks to the bottom of the standpipes. Even though gravity provides an unfailing source of backup fuel pressure in most cases, a standby electric fuel boost pump is installed to meet certification requirements in certain attitudes. Its use is not required for takeoffs and landings. Many of the Cutlass RGs had the optional refueling steps and handles installed on the forward fuselage, allowing the lithe of limb to scale the heights to check fuel level during preflight.

Slimmer doorposts to improve visibility were introduced with the Cutlass RG, part of 1980's package of changes for the 172-series; though there have been some reports of increased cracks in this area, as compared with the older, thicker doorposts. The cabin's huge entrance doors allow easy boarding from either side of the aircraft. However, to get in one has to perch on the slim rubber pad atop the main gear strut and stretch a foot into the cabin. Alternately, a long-legged individual can bypass the strut pad and vault directly into the saddle from the ground. A fixed entrance step hanging from the side of the fuselage would have been a welcome addition. As with all of the four-place Cessnas, the front seat passengers board first, sliding their seats forward to increase boarding room for the rear riders. A forward-hinging door on the left side of the fuselage opens onto the baggage compartment, rated for 200 pounds, including the 50 pounds allowable on a shelf in the tailcone, above the wheel-well. The ELT is located on the side of the baggage compartment wall, on the rear shelf.

The large dorsal fin and vertical tail maintain acceptable directional stability, even without the keel effect from the landing gear. The rudder can be trimmed by an adjustable bungee as well as by a ground-adjustable tab, and a large trim tab is found on the right elevator. The Cutlass RG employs a tight gap between the horizontal stabilizer and elevator to enhance pitch control at slow speed. The battery access cover is on the left side of the tailcone.

On Board Room

Finding no surprises on the walkaround, we climb into the cockpit to encounter a mixture of Skyhawk and Centurion architecture. The landing gear control is a massive handle, rather than a delicate switch, and an extra vernier knob is provided for the propeller pitch control. The emergency hand pump for the gear system is in the floor between the pilot seats, giving notice that this is a real, live complex airplane. However, the throttle is a familiar push-pull knob, and the control wheel is a slim yoke from the Skyhawk.

The tall, well-arranged panel places the avionics master switch and circuit breakers on the left sidewall, with the remainder of the switches and CBs on the pilot's subpanel. Engine gauges are clustered in front of the pilot, and the sacred-six flight instruments and a stack of three radio navigation instruments also fit nicely onto the pilot's side of the panel, leaving only miscellaneous instruments like the EGT and carb temp gauge on the right, along with the glove box. For shorter pilots, the crank-up seat option is needed to improve the view over the nose. Another worthwhile option is the one for overhead skylight windows, adding visibility in the blind spot above the cabin while turning.

The vertical central console does not intrude upon the floor space. It carries the elevator and rudder trim wheels, cowl flaps control, and fuel selector with "left," "right" or "both" positions. A stack of 300-series Cessna/ARC avi-

The Cutlass RG panel looks like that of a well-equipped Skyhawk, except for the gear lever, prop control and rudder trim wheel. The Cessna/ARC avionics were adequate but are often replaced to improve resale value.

onics was in the middle of the panel of our sample airplane; it incorporated an audio panel with marker beacon receiver, dual RT-385A incandescent-readout nav-comm radios, with glideslope displayed on number 1 and automatic radial centering on the number 2 nav head for monitoring progress with an off-side VOR. An RT-395A transponder and encoder, an R546E ADF and a 200A single-axis autopilot completed the factory-installed list, the typical Cessna-installed "Cutlass RG II with Nav-Pac" equipment package. By now, most 1980s Cessnas have been retrofitted with newer radios.

The installed load of gear brought the empty weight up to 1,666 pounds, leaving but 620 pounds for cabin payload with the tanks topped off. Carrying four 170-pound persons would only have lowered the fuel load by ten gallons, however, still a more than ample endurance of over five hours. The Cutlass RG does not share the Skyhawk's certification in both utility and normal categories, having only a normal-category loading envelope and stress limits of 3.8 Gs positive and 1.52 Gs negative.

Starting procedure begins with confirming cowl flaps open and gear handle down; a squat switch on the nose-gear strut supposedly inhibits power-pack operation, but why tempt fate? Firing up the simple, carburetor-equipped Cutlass RG is a matter of flipping on the battery and alternator rockers, pumping the throttle a couple of times or priming a few strokes in cold weather, then twisting the key to crank. For hot starts, the boost pump may be turned on to purge vapor locks. The big-bore Lyc shakes off its slumber and barks obediently into an idle. Releasing the parking brake handle, we added power to taxi, enjoying light pedal pressures but sluggish control, due to the indirect Cessna nose wheel steering that uses springs for steering.

Runup is performed at 1,800 rpm (there is no yellow arc on the tachometer to avoid), where mags, carb heat, propeller pitch and engine gauges are checked. Control movement is easily confirmed through the wall of windows surrounding the cockpit, even to the rear. The doors and windows are snugged tightly shut, although if one pops open inflight it may be closed with no particular difficulty; not only do the side windows prop open for ground ventilation, they can be opened inflight up to the 164-knot redline. The fuel boost pump is turned on momentarily to confirm a rise in fuel pressure, then left off unless the pressure falls below .5 PSI. Wing flaps are left up unless the runway surface is soft or rough; in that case, 10° are set to hasten the liftoff, but only if the aircraft's takeoff weight is 2,550 pounds or less. Evidently the limited horsepower is not capable of accelerating the extra drag of flaps at the heavier weight.

Getaway Time

Full power brings the O-360 up to a very un-Skyhawk-like snarl as the constant-speed propeller digs in at 2,700 rpm. At light weight, acceleration is rapid and a characteristically powerful Cessna elevator allows the nose to be lightened early in the run. Rotating at 55 knots normally, the liftoff comes at 60 to 65 knots, using about 1,000 to 1,200 feet of runway. As with the rest of the 172 series, the Cutlass RG is takeoff limited, being capable of landing in spaces shorter than it is possible to take off from.

V_Y comes at 84 knots, V_X at 67 knots. Once the goatsucker nose-gear doors are cycled closed the climb rate builds to 800–900 fpm at sea level elevations. With power back to 25-square, climb deteriorates to 700 fpm or so, with 500 fpm more typical as altitude increases. In cruise, the Cutlass RG does its best work above 5,000 feet, where the thinner air lessens drag on the large airframe and the throttle can be fully open at cruise manifold pressure. At higher altitudes it will be necessary to increase rpm beyond the 2,500 step in the green arc to achieve 75% power, with an attendant swell in noise level.

The Cutlass RG is in its element at cross-country cruise. The view of the world passing under one's wings is superb, the cabin is relatively spacious and well lit by the ample windows, and the noise level is moderate at 2,400 to 2,500 rpm. Handling is responsive but not touchy; rudder is not needed for normal turns once at cruise. In climb or slowflight, of course, a twist of the rudder trim wheel will ease the strain on one's right leg.

Cruise speed indications at middle altitudes is 120 knots, or roughly 131 knots TAS, using 24-square power, about 68%. Owners typically plan for a

Popular as a viceless complex trainer, many Cutlass RGs have seen extensive service with flight schools.

135-knot cruise speed, using 65 to 70% power and burning 9.5 to 10 gallons per hour. Should IFR be needed, the Cutlass RG with full tanks has the ability to fly four hours with good alternate and reserve fuel.

Slowing down to find the Skyhawk heritage, the Cutlass RG can decelerate with the best of them; the gear can go out at speeds up 140 knots, which is seldom seen in normal cruise, and once it is down there is no speed limitation other than the aircraft's red line. The first 10° of flap can go down below 130 knots, the rest of the flaps being allowed below 100. We chugged around at 40 knots in dirty configuration while holding altitude, normal Skyhawk performance. Stalls are typical Cessna; a warning sounds about 5 knots before the break, which comes at 50 knots power-off in clean configuration, 45 knots when dirty. No nasty habits manifest themselves, and one is flying again as soon as the yoke is moved forward.

Landings are easy, if one remembers the Cutlass' nose-high stance while parked and pulls the wheel all the way back, rather than allowing the airplane to land on the nose wheel. Confirming that the gear is down is a simple matter of looking out the cabin window to see if a wheel is there. A 70-knot approach with power at 17 inches or so keeps the pattern manageable, and slowing to 65 knots when the last of the flaps go down on final allows plenty of time for a power-off flare and touchdown. A 1,000-foot turnoff is easy to achieve.

The Cutlass RG is a real pussycat of a high-performance retractable, and yet its 130–140 cruise speed and long legs are far from the worst in its category. It shares the normal aging-Cessna weaknesses, so a pre-purchase inspection could be handled by just about any shop familiar with Cessnas. The main gear pivots and attaching hardware have been subject to failure, resulting in landing with a trailing gear, so that area requires attention. Early Cutlass RGs should also be inspected carefully for signs of corrosion before purchase; Cessna's painting procedures were hit-and-miss in the early 1980s.

All and all, however, a simple powerplant and proven airframe make the Cutlass RG relatively economical to keep in the air. As with its parent, the ubiquitous 172, it does nothing spectacularly, but manages to do everything comfortably and well. As a Skyhawk pilot, you can step up to a Cutlass RG and feel like you've never left home.

8 ▪ Flying with Water Wings
The Unique Lake Buccaneer

If you're interested in owning a light retractable that's a little, well, different, a Lake Buccaneer should fill the bill. For one thing it's the only one of the group that can make more than one water landing! And as an amphibious airplane, the fuselage doubles as a boat hull, enabling one appliance to combine the fun of both worlds—flying and boating.

Lakes have a long, long history, tracing back to the post-war euphoria of 1946, when Grumman's David Thurston and Republic Aircraft's Herbert Lindblad teamed up to design the Skimmer, a 3-place, 150-hp flying boat. The Colonial Aircraft C-1 Skimmer was finally certificated on September 19, 1955. After 24 were built, the installation of a 180-hp Lycoming engine created the C-2 Skimmer IV and the side-facing third seat was exchanged for a conventional two-place bench; the C-2 received certification on December 24, 1957; 118 were built. After new ownership reorganized as Lake Aircraft, a follow-on

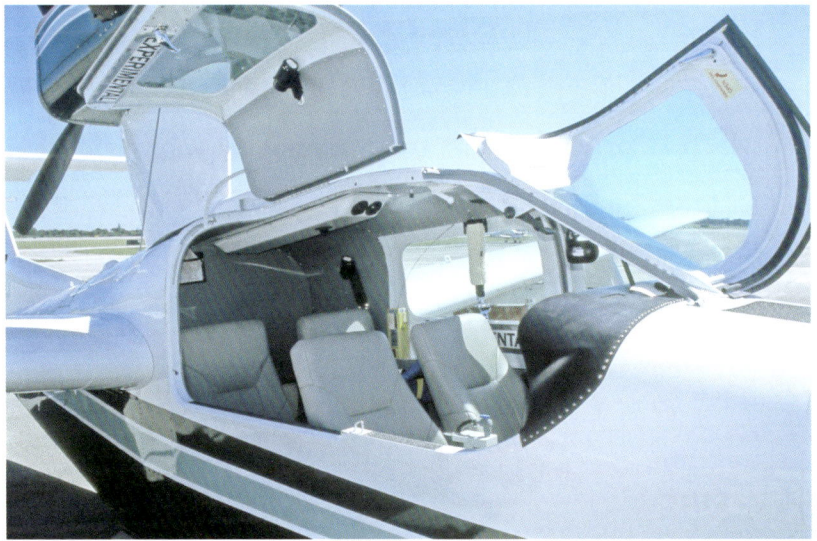

The five/six place Lake Renegade has a large hatch on the right side of the cabin to facilitate reaching the rear seats. The swing-over windshield is standard for all the Lake airplanes, allowing boarding from over the nose or dockside.

As a dual-purpose aircraft, the Lake Buccaneer must be built heavier for the punishment of water operation, with a high-mounted engine and tail.

LA-4 was certified on July 26, 1960, still powered with the 180-hp Lycoming but with a 17-inch longer bow that enclosed the formerly-protruding nose wheel/bumper. Two feet were added to each wingtip and a foot more length to each aileron. Gross weight went from 2,350 to 2,400 pounds.

After approximately 200 of the LA-4s were built, the 200-hp LA-4-200 Buccaneer was certificated on 26 May 1970, with a gross weight increase to 2,600 pounds. The lighter 180-hp version was phased out in 1971 and roughly 650 of the LA-4-200s were built through 1987, acquiring another 90 pounds of gross weight along the way. The stretched six-place 250-hp Lake Renegade appeared in 1984 and soon replaced the Buccaneer.

While marginal as a four-seater, the Lake offers capability matched by no other 200-hp retractable. As a floating airplane, most of the working parts are located high above normal landplane position; the entrance doors, for instance, are hinged sections of the windshield, allowing dry-footed entrance when nosed into a beach by clambering over the bow. On land, a step onto the spray-rail reaches the cabin, bathtub style, and climbing from the gunwales to the wing root and cabin roof reaches the pylon-mounted pusher engine. The cruciform tail is needed to avoid submersing the elevators during takeoff.

We were originally introduced to Lake flying by Bob Billingsley of Afton, Oklahoma, who flew and instructed in the Buccaneers for decades. Parked on dry land, a Lake requires some athleticism for preflight. As Billingsley showed me around his company's 1977 Lake, he pointed out the seven vital drain plugs, five in the hull compartments and one in each wingtip float; these are removed with a hex wrench which also opens up many other things, such as the hydraulic system filler plug. He has an electric bilge pump installed, but says there is very little need for it with daily haul-outs. The pump's outlet is on the left side of the fuselage under the wing root, near the two fuel quick drains. The hull's bottom is constructed of .051 75ST aluminum sheeting.

The fuel system is a single 40-gallon bladder cell behind the cabin with optional 7.5-gallon tanks available for the wingtip floats. Billingsley did not opt for the aux tanks, primarily because their use is prohibited during water operations. The on/off fuel valve is on the aft cabin wall.

The 200-hp Lycoming IO-360-A1B swings a pusher-type constant-speed propeller and the cowling is open at the rear for the cooling air exhaust to exit. This makes it important to preflight for loose objects that could migrate into the propeller. Even though we made the test flight in 90-degree temperatures, we never saw the CHT above 250°F, so engine cooling seems to be good. The front of the cowling swings up to reveal the accessory section and the oil dipstick. There's a catch basin for the crankcase breather line, to be emptied periodically. Otherwise, the breather tube would drip excess oil onto the pristine white deck below. The well-braced pylon structure is stressed for 37 Gs, well in excess of certification requirements.

The Lake's long wings are responsible for much of its performance, in that water planes must take off and land at relatively slow speeds, both to limit the shock of impacting waves and to reach liftoff before encountering the barrier of water drag. Hydraulically-actuated flaps cover 70% of the wingspan, but extend only to 20 degrees, as their primary purpose is to create extra lift. Landing lights are located at mid-span on the left wing's leading edge and the pitot tube is on the left wingtip.

The leggy main landing gear uses a soft trailing-link geometry, retracting hydraulically into open wells in the wing. Its 11-foot-wide stance gives ample stability. The nose gear folds forward into the bow, behind enclosing doors; no, they don't seal watertight but do provide some drag reduction aloft and afloat. The nose wheel does not steer, so brakes are needed for land maneuvering. Gerdes brakes, wheels and struts are standard, with Cleveland brakes optional. There are no safety squat-switches on the gear, since it must be waterproofed for retraction while afloat, but the gear handle on the hydraulic powerpack must be pulled out before it can be moved, thus providing a measure of protection.

Wide wings give the Buccaneer the ability to lift off at slow speed and land in short spaces.

The airplane's CG is near the step and with the cabin empty the nose wheel can easily be picked up by the prow for ground handling. If flown solo, ballast must be carried in the bow locker to maintain balance. While the useful load is a respectable 1,000 pounds or so, there is little space in which to put it. Four persons are a snug fit, the overall cabin length is 62.5 inches and the baggage hold behind the seats is long and slim. The bow compartment is used for anchor and line stowage. But the little airplane does offer amphibious capability at a price far below converted landplanes and handles very well on the water.

All control surfaces are pushrod actuated, other than for aileron cables in the cabin area. The trim tabs on the horizontal stabilizer aren't really tabs, but are hydraulically-actuated flippers outboard of the elevators. These stabilizer flippers adjust to trim the aircraft directly instead of by displacing the elevators, hence they operate over a much wider range than a trim tab. For precise water handling, a spring-loaded water rudder is extended from the bottom of the air rudder.

Beyond the usual nicks and dings normally acquired in handling a mid-wing flying boat, Billingsley has not experienced many maintenance difficulties. The Lake does require constant attention to minor repairs, he says, and it helps to be mechanically inclined. He pronounced the airplane easy to work on, except for a few areas of the engine installation. Because of the engine's distance from the cockpit, an optional 9,400-BTU Southwind combustion heater is installed atop the cabin, just forward of the engine pylon.

All Aboard for the Launching

Preflight familiarization accomplished, it was time to mount up and go down the ramp. Climbing into the 44.5-inch wide cabin, we found an IFR panel and avionics stack, although most Lake missions are VFR, and a different sort of cockpit arrangement. The engine controls are hung from the overhead instead of mounted on the subpanel and the gear, flap levers and emergency hydraulic hand pump are on the center console. A water rudder control and a stowed paddle show that this is not an ordinary retractable.

Starting requires the normal Lycoming fuel injection technique, running the boost pump long enough to bring fuel up to the engine's flow divider, then

The long Lake main gear leg folds into the underside of the wing and uses trailing-link geometry for smoother touchdowns. Brakes are essential for steering.

The Lake instrument panel is bereft of power controls, which are located overhead. The hydraulic system operates the gear, flaps, trim surfaces and brakes. This modern panel is installed in a 270-hp turbocharged Sea Wolf version of the larger Lake Renegade.

cranking with mixture lean until achieving a light-off. The distant bark of the aft-mounted engine announces success.

We performed the mags and prop check before entering the water, while we still had brakes. We then rolled down the incline and the Lake once more was bobbing in its element. The gear was stowed and water rudder extended as we taxied slowly at idle power to a takeoff lane. The waterline is only a foot or so below one's elbow, very much a part of the Lake experience.

After the Lake was allowed to weathercock into the wind, flaps were checked full down, boost pump switched on, and the water rudder was raised. Billingsley then moved the overhead throttle full forward, holding the wheel back to bring the Lake up "out of the hole" and onto the step (which the airplane reaches very quickly with a light load). We planed along on the step for perhaps a quarter mile to reach the 60-mph liftoff speed, that magic moment when the spanking of the waves ceases and the transformation to an airplane is complete. Billingsley says no-flap takeoffs are not possible, as it takes almost 85 mph to lift off and the airplane just cannot reach that speed because of water drag. We climbed out showing 600 fpm at 80 mph with flaps down, transitioning to a 25-square cruise climb at 100 mph with the flaps up. This delivered a 400 fpm rate of climb. The best rate-of-climb speed is 85 mph, flaps up, while best angle comes at 60 with flaps down.

Billingsley leveled out at 1,000 feet or so, his normal sightseeing altitude, and cruised at 24/2400, roughly 70% power, to show 125 mph IAS, a true airspeed of about 130 mph. Speed is not the Lake's strong suit, with a relatively large airframe and modest power, but the factory claims 150 mph at 8,000 feet MSL. Billingsley says there are significant variations between airplanes built at different times, and some Lakes are just faster than others. The view from the forward seating position is superb, impeded only by the long bow section ahead. Control feel at cruise is well balanced, albeit a little on the heavy side, and the hydraulic trim lever must be held in position to move the flippers, because it's a valve, not a direct control.

We pulled up another 2,000 feet to take a break from low flying and to check out the Lake's docile stall characteristics. With no flaps, the stall buffet occurred at 75 mph, delaying to 55 with flaps down. The gear has no effect on stall speed. A departure stall with full power produced only a rocking motion with the wheel full aft at 50 mph, and no true stall break occurred. So, a climb-out over obstacles can be made by feel alone, by just pulling back until the buffet starts then easing off a bit.

We also explored the Lake's noted reversed pitch response to power changes. Due to the high-mounted pusher engine, increasing power causes the nose to drop while pulling power back brings the nose up—the reverse of normal airplanes. For this reason a hurried go-around from a bounced water touchdown is not recommended—the sudden increase in power could force the nose down and induce a porpoise. But, with anticipation, we found the trim change easily managed, although noticeable.

In flight, the Lake is fairly noisy despite the engine's remote location. The upper cabin area is constructed of fiberglass and Plexiglas, neither of which have much sound-deadening qualities. The ride is a bit active for the passengers, due to the forward position of the cabin in relation to the center of gravity.

Impressed by the tales of my vast (half vast, anyway) water flying experience, Billingsley decided to let me splash through a takeoff and landing, and we looked for a convenient, roomy spot. The Lake draws only about a foot of water, so it can operate in some marginal areas if there is no floating trash. We found a channel a couple of miles long, between towering limestone bluffs, wide enough to avoid boat traffic. Bob stressed the need for a pre-landing drill by saying "this is a water landing, the gear is UP," to avoid a disastrous gear-down landing on water. A small mirror is mounted on the left wingtip float to check the nose-gear doors' position visually.

Slowing to 125 mph, flaps were selected down to set up an 80 mph approach—in this airplane a power-off glide provides a comfortable approach angle. Leveling out with our hip pockets just off the water, we allowed the airplane to settle on level for a step landing, much like a wheel landing in a taildragger landplane. As airspeed dropped off, I used 18 inches of manifold pressure to hold 35 mph (the airspeed indicator goes down to 20), a good step-taxi speed. Then we practiced ruddering the airplane around in skidding step turns, a maneuver sure to make any landlubber cringe in anticipation of a ground loop. It is necessary to keep the wingtip floats out of the water during step taxiing, as they can be damaged by a hard impact with the water. Takeoff is simply a matter of opening the throttle and accelerating to 60 mph.

During climb-out, I reduced rpm to 2,500 after retracting flaps and re-marked at how quickly the prop governor responded to my touch. "That's be-cause you're moving the mixture control," Billingsley countered as we charged toward the 100-foot tall cliffs at the end of the channel. Now I know the difference between a knob and a lever; but the overhead controls are quite convenient to use, once learned.

The Lake actually lands on water in a similar fashion to landing a sail-plane; both types of aircraft place the pilot forward of a shoulder-mounted wing and require careful use of the controls to touch down and decelerate in a flat, wings-level attitude. Takeoffs and landings on land are quite short, about 700 feet for takeoff roll and less than a thousand feet for landing rollout.

Billingsley feels that the Lake is ideally suited to its mission, due to its versatility and the magnificent view from the cockpit. At the same time, he missed a high-wing seaplane's ability to dock safely just about anywhere. The Lake cannot be docked in certain wind and current conditions and is always prone to damage at the pier unless carefully tended, Billingsley says. Rough water landings are also a marginal area because the Lake's 38-foot wingspan makes it such a good glider in the air and the flat step portion of the hull makes it equally buoyant on the water. The light wing loading increases the difficulty of dropping the airplane into the water with precision and the hull leaves the craft on the step entirely too long after touchdown for comfort.

Compromises are part of aircraft design, and the Lake is necessarily bur-dened with the weight of extra structure and the drag of tip floats and a big wing. That said, nothing else ever quite did its job on relatively minimal horse-power, so if you're into boating as well as flying, why not combine the two for double the fun?

9 · Piper's Comanche 180
A Thoroughly Modern Antique

Even though the last Piper Comanche 180 was built in 1964, it won't look out of place when you tie it down next to the newer light retractable-gear airplanes. Quite simply, its sleek lines and comfortable cabin belie its mid-1950s origin. To place the Piper PA-24 design in perspective, you must remember that it originated in an era dominated by fabric-covered Piper Tri-Pacers and taildragger Cessna 180s and 170s, a time of grass runways and Spartan airport facilities.

After the smashing success of the Tri-Pacer and Apache in the early 1950s, Piper's plans for continued conquest of the business and personal aircraft market called for a high-performance single, one bridging the gap between the pedestrian Tri-Pacer and the twin-engine Apache. Luckily, the folks at Lycoming engines, Piper's neighbors a few miles down the river, were about to introduce a larger four-cylinder powerplant, a growth version of the 150-hp O-320 called the O-360, and Piper's engineers went to work on an airplane to utilize this new 180-hp engine.

As its design evolved, Lycoming unveiled plans for a six-cylinder version of the O-360, using the same pistons and cylinder barrels, so the Comanche was quickly adapted to use the new 250-hp engine as well, later increased to 260-hp. Eventually, the eight-cylinder, 400-hp IO-720 engine was stuffed into the airframe, as well as a 260-hp twin-turboed version of the IO-540, and the Twin Comanche derivative was a winner in its own right. There was even, believe it or not, a Comanche 260 seaplane, mounted on EDO 2700 floats! But, our focus remains on light retractables, hence we'll review the PA-24-180.

The 180-hp Comanche was the first of the line, achieving certification on June 20, 1957, nearly eight months before the Comanche 250 was certified. The two powerplant options were built concurrently until mid-1964, but the 180 was never as popular as the 250, and production of the Comanche 180 was ended after 1,143 examples were built. The final 8 years of Comanche production used only the six-cylinder engine. As the Cherokee line grew in the 1960s, a simpler-to-build retractable-gear version of the Cherokee 180, introduced in 1967 as the Cherokee Arrow, took over the light retractable slot in the Piper line, and we'll cover that airplane in the following chapter.

All Comanche production was finally brought to a halt in 1972, when the surging floodwaters of Hurricane Agnes inundated the Lock Haven airport and filled Piper's plant almost to the ceiling. The disaster presented an opportunity for reassessment, and the corporate owners that had taken over from the Piper family deemed that the slow-selling Comanche was no longer competitive and would not be returned to production.

As a light four-place retractable, the Comanche 180 was a fine blend of economy and comfort, offering reasonable performance in a good looking package; it is quite possibly the most beautiful airplane ever built by the practical Piper company. Often maligned as an underpowered dog, mostly by persons who have never so much as sat in one, the Comanche 180 does remarkably well when flown within its limitations. True, it isn't a load-hauler like the Comanche 250/260, but every airplane comes with a set of weight and balance papers, and if you observe its restrictions the airplane will meet or exceed the handbook specs.

The stories of underpowered Comanche 180s may stem from persons who fail to take note of the airplane's inability to carry full tanks of gas and four husky passengers with luggage without going over gross weight. Yes, the airframe may be good for it, but the performance charts become meaningless. In addition, the laminar flow wing section doesn't respond to "horse it into the air" treatment as well as the old Clark-Y airfoils used in other Piper products, and this may have helped fuel rumors that the Comanche was underpowered.

The Comanche was an innovative airplane for its time; only the Mooney Mark 20 predated it in the light retractable field. It incorporated such advanced features as all-metal stressed-skin construction and an all-flying stabilator tail. To preserve its Tri-Pacer heritage, however, the Comanche used the familiar overhead trim crank and a hand lever for simultaneous application of wheel brakes.

When we were looking around for a subject airplane to evaluate, we ran across a 1960 Comanche 180 owned by Jim Breckenridge of Rich Hill, Missouri. Breckenridge had formerly owned a Cherokee 180 and was ready to step up to a light retractable when he began to look for a replacement for his Cherokee. He spotted the 180 with 3,300 hours on the airframe and 700 hours on a Mattituck-overhauled engine, and it was love at first sight. The overhead trim, small plunger-type throttle knob, hand brake and double-latching door were all familiar touches from his Cherokee, so the transition was a snap.

Resplendent in a shiny red, white and blue Imron paint job, the plane certainly didn't look as if she were "over thirty." To judge its age, however, take note of the airplane's 6.00 x 6 nose wheel tire, another feature borrowed from the Tri-Pacer. During the 1950s, the majority of general aviation airports were unpaved, necessitating rugged, high-flotation landing gear. Along with the tire size, all three of the Comanche's wheels, forks and struts are identical. One worthwhile mod involves exchanging the main landing gear's double forks for the late-style single-fork gear legs, relocating the brake discs to the

The Comanche's stabilator was the first wide-spread general aviation use of an "all-flying" tail. A wide anti-servo trim tab spans most of the trailing edge.

inside of the wheel-well and eliminating quite a bit of hardware that hangs out in the breeze.

The electrically-operated landing gear zips up or down in about seven seconds, nestling into open gear wells with only small doors to cover the struts. Rubber bungee cords, requiring replacement at 500-hour intervals, are used in the system to assure over-center latching. A squat switch to inhibit ground retraction is on the left main gear strut. Manual extension is provided by a telescoping handle on the cockpit floor that is man-handled through a vertical arc much like the manual gear handle of the early Mooneys. The compressed emergency handle moves through a fore-and-aft arc with each normal cycle of the landing gear, so one must not place charts or books on the floor between the seats, which could restrict gear operation.

The long Comanche snout is fitted with a simple hinged cowling, enabling the pilot to lay the engine room bare by opening three latches with wing-nut equipped Dzus fasteners. Removing the nosecap, however, will require demounting the constant speed Hartzell (or McCauley) propeller. The four-cylinder O-360 seems impossibly small, crowded into the very front of a long engine compartment that is roomy for even the O-540-series engine. The 1958 and 1959 airplanes had a square air filter housing under their chin, unlike the rounded inlet on the later versions. Small inlet scoops on the lower

The relatively-short Comanche landing gear used 6.00 x 6 tires all around. Double-fork main gear legs denote the early Comanches; a square induction air opening was used on the 1958 and 1959 airplanes, but this 1960 model has the round air intake.

cowl feed cabin air vents on the firewall. No cowl flaps are fitted, nor is a separate oil-checking access door provided.

The fuel system consists of 30-gallon bladder tanks in each wing, a capacity initially designed to accommodate the O-540 engine. By filling the tanks only to the bottom of the vacuum-bottle filler openings, fuel can be limited to 50 gallons, which is more than ample for the O-360. The lack of quick-drains for the tanks would be shocking to pilots of more modern airplanes; the only drain originally provided was a strainer drain located inside a door under the belly. At the time, few airplanes were fitted with spring-loaded sump drains in their fuel tanks; most, like the Comanche, simply had safety-wired pipe plugs in the sumps. Like all aircraft with bladder fuel cells, the Comanche should be stored with the tanks topped to prevent deterioration from drying out. The tanks typically rot away at the tops first, so before purchasing any Comanche it would be well to fill it to maximum capacity and let it sit overnight to check for leaks.

The tapered high-aspect ratio PA-24 wing is an elegant departure from the Tri-Pacer or Apache slabs. A modified NACA 64_2 A215, it was Piper's first foray into laminar-flow airfoils, which were just coming into use in general aviation with the Mooney and Helio, and it is flush riveted back to the main spar

The large cowling half can be raised for inspection without tools; the 180-hp O-360 engine occupies only a fraction of the space available.

to assure attached airflow. Its maximum thickness is far enough aft to allow the main spars to pass through the cabin under the edge of the rear seat, where they are bolted together for maximum strength. At one time there was an AD requiring cutting out a section of the wing skin to inspect the spar on airplanes with over 1,500 hours time in service, but few cracks were found and the AD was later rescinded. Another AD, still in force, requires inspection of the fuel tanks and underwing vents periodically unless retrofitted anti-icing vents are installed. The wing's leading edge is swept sharply aft near the wing roots, which contain the fuel cells; small airflow-control plates nestle in the corner where the swept leading edge transitions to a straight outboard portion.

The Comanche 180 was one of the last airplanes certificated under CAR 3 (Civil Air Regulation Part 3) with no artificial stall warning system at all; a plate in the left leading edge showed where the vane would have been located had our test bird been a Comanche 250. A fixed trim tab is on the left aileron. Landing lights are located in the leading edge near each wingtip, where they do an excellent job of illuminating the edges of the runway; Breckenridge reports a "black hole" directly ahead, however.

A 200-pound capacity baggage compartment is located aft of the right wing root, reached through a forward-hinged door that requires a key for opening (the first 102 PA-24s were restricted to 100 pounds of baggage). A 12-volt battery is mounted in the aft fuselage behind the baggage compartment. Static air ports are located on the sides of the rear fuselage. A scoop

The 200-pound baggage compartment behind the rear seats is reached through this door above the Comanche's wing-walk.

on the top of the aft fuselage feeds an overhead vent system; this change was added in mid-1959 to enhance airflow, in addition to the original Tri-Pacer-style adjustable vents in the cabin sidewalls at each seat and the firewall vents.

The Comanche's all-moving horizontal tail was another radical departure for 1958; only the Helio Courier had used a stabilator previously in general aviation. Piper went on to use the stabilator in nearly all of its lighter aircraft, up through the Aztec twin. A wide anti-servo tab provides feel as well as trimming functions. The generous fin and rudder stretch up to 7.5 feet above the tarmac; the Comanche 180 did not require retrofitting of the "goose-egg" rudder balance weights in 1974, now seen on all Comanche 250 and 260s, although the 180's V_{NE} was reduced from 202 to 188 mph.

Boarding requires a moderate step-up onto the wing walk on the right wing; so short were the Comanche's main gear oleo struts that no step was provided. The door has an auxiliary latch at the top rear corner, in addition to the lower latch in the middle of the frame. Entrance to the cockpit is relatively simple, particularly if the right front seat is pushed aft to widen the path to the left seat. Sliding across the cabin into the pilot's seat, we note the floor mounted fuel selector, the emergency gear lever, the hand brake lever hanging down under the panel and a large nose-gear wheel-well extending aft into the cabin. In addition to the pitch trim on the ceiling, a rudder trim knob under the panel adjusts yaw pressures. By 1961, toe brakes were standard for the pilot's rudder pedals, with the central hand brake retained for the copilot.

The instrument panel shows the Comanche 180's age. The arrangement of the instruments is haphazard, designed more for convenience and style than a good scan pattern. An improved panel with center-stacked radios, introduced in 1961, helped somewhat, but the instrument placement was still non-standard. Old-style J&H gyros from World War II were still being installed as new equipment in 1960. The controls and switches across the lower panel were a curiously antiquated lot as well. The starter is engaged by a proper chrome push-button, not a twist-key switch. The mixture control is an unguarded red knob to the left of the throttle, about where newer airplanes would have their carburetor heat control (naturally, that item is found on the right side of the panel), and the propeller pitch knob, next to the diminutive throttle, is a massive device that looks like a steam valve from a boiler.

Flaps are lowered by yanking on a three-position handle near the nose-gear wheel-well, extending to a maximum of 27 degrees (the larger Comanches soon offered electric flaps extending to 32 degrees). The left-right-off fuel selector is mounted in a dog-dish on the floor between the seats; its L-shaped handle forms a schematic diagram of the fuel flow. The emergency gear extension lever is engaged by removing an access plate on the floor and unlatching the gear linkage prior to extending the handle.

The test airplane's avionics were installed on both sides of the panel, including the space where a glove compartment originally resided. In the Comanche's youth, tube-type radios required a rack full of remote power supplies and amplifier boxes in the tailcone, but today's updated PA-24s will have had those items stripped out. The equipped weight of our test airplane was 1,567 pounds, which translates to 608 pounds of cabin payload with full fuel tanks. In most cases, however, one can get by with 50 gallons of fuel, bringing payload up by 60 pounds, enough for four persons averaging 167 pounds each.

Ready to Cast Off

We prepared to crank up and go flying. Because there's a separate starter button, the O-360 is usually started on the left magneto to take advantage of its impulse spring. We pumped the throttle twice and pressed the big chrome

The 1960 Comanche 180's instrument panel reflects the standards of the time; standard-T instrument layouts had not yet come into vogue and the carburetor heat and mixture controls are reversed over modern placement. The pull handle near the pilot's right knee is the brake lever (there are no toe brakes) and the tall vertical lever is for the flaps.

The Comanche 180 looks as good as it flies, still a sought-after light retractable even in middle age.

button. Somewhere out in front, at the end of the long prow, the four-cylinder Lycoming woke from its slumbers and settled into a smooth idle. Switching magnetos to "both," the basic avionics and lights are turned on. Unless the airplane has been retrofitted with an alternator, one avoids turning on unnecessary electrical drain while taxiing because the DC generator only produces current above 1,200 rpm, leaving much of the taxi load to the battery.

The direct-linked nose wheel steering is positive, with firm rudder pressures needed to turn the 6.00 x 6 nose tire. The relatively long wheelbase makes tight taxi turns difficult, particularly with the lack of individual toe brakes. A positive parking brake locks the wheels for the runup, leaving the pilot's hands free for cockpit duties. Other than the need for cycling the constant speed propeller to check pitch change, the pre-takeoff checklist is no longer than that of a Cherokee. Magnetos are checked at 2,000 rpm, the carburetor heat is tested, the boost pump is switched on for takeoff, the trim crank is adjusted to neutral and the door's two latches are checked. Controls free and instruments set, we lined up for departure.

We were loaded to about 2,250 pounds for takeoff, so the acceleration was rapid and the airplane was ready to fly by the time it reached 60 mph, about 800 ft down the runway (with the aid of a 10-knot wind). As the gear retracted, the full-power climb rate built up to 1,000 fpm at the 96 mph V_Y. Normal climb power of 25 inches and 2,500 rpm gave us 800 fpm, and the rate was still 750 fpm as we leveled off at 4,000 feet, where the throttle was full open at 25 inches.

The willing little Lycoming produced 75% power at 23 inches and 2,400 rpm, resulting in an indicated airspeed of 142 mph, for a true airspeed of 152 mph (132 knots) on a fuel burn of about 10 gph. Backing off a bit to 22 inches, or about 70%, we saw 139 mph, a true of 149 mph (129 knots), and a quiet 21 inches at 2,100 rpm, a bit less than 60% power, gave us 130 mph IAS, truing out at 139 mph (121 kts) on about 8 gph. The light Comanche controls stiffen up somewhat at cruise speed, but the airplane is still lighter and more responsive than many of the more modern designs. The trim crank needs only a nudge to adjust pitch attitude and rudder trim is equally sensitive.

We found the noise level pleasantly low, even at maximum cruise, probably due to the long distance between the cabin and the engine. Visibility is mid-50s style, meaning that the low window line and slim windshield leave several blind spots to be cleared before doing maneuvers. Breckenridge reports that the fuel management is easier than with the Cherokee, with less wing-heaviness due to fuel imbalance thanks to the wing root fuel tanks. At the 10-gph fuel consumption, the Comanche 180 can range out to 700 miles or more with plenty of reserve. A few late models, after serial number 2,300, can have the 250's auxiliary tanks—and with 90 gallons on board, an endurance that is practically unendurable.

Slowed down to 60 mph indicated in clean configuration, the Comanche still hung on under full control, but any further reduction brought on the unmistakable buffeting of an imminent stall. We brought the power to idle and got a stall break at the same 60 mph, recovering easily in less than 200 feet. With gear and flaps extended, the stall buffet began at 60 and a sharp stall occurred at 55 mph IAS; we ate up 300 feet in that recovery.

Upon our return to the field, we intercepted the ILS to observe the airplane's manners on the gauges; we found the Comanche to be quite stable on the glideslope at 120 mph, with the gear down and 18 inches of m.p. The gear can be extended below 150 mph, normally well above cruise speed, and the flaps can be lowered below 125 mph. There is the normal low-wing pitchdown with flaps extended, easily adjusted with a twist of the trim. Boost pump on and mixture rich, we had only to push in the propeller knob for the transition to a landing. New-to-type Comanche pilots must remind themselves of the three-position gear switch, which has a neutral detent between up and down for manual extensions. Also, the amber "gear up" and green "gear down" lights dim automatically when the navigation lights are turned on, leading to panic on the next daytime flight if the nav lights are left on.

In the traffic pattern, we used about 90 mph with a notch of flaps while maneuvering to the base leg, adding more flap on base and final. We slowed to 80 mph as we rolled onto final, with 75 mph over the numbers, and we still floated 400 feet or so before touching down in a "flown on" landing. On a short field approach we crossed the fence at 70 mph and touched down with the wheel fully back. We soon learned not to try for a full-stall landing, because the laminar-flow wing paid off with little warning, and the nose wheel plunked down with a thump as soon as the tail stalled. Turning around in 1,400 feet of runway was easily possible.

Despite the draginess of its airframe, the Comanche 180 turns in good performance in relative comfort. The age of the design calls for some dedication on the part of the owner; new parts may require a little sleuthing, and the need for periodic replacement of fuel cells, landing gear bungee cords, and door seals add to the upkeep chores. However, the Comanche's factory-standard zinc chromating keeps corrosion to a minimum. The AD list is lengthy, and many require recurring inspections; the wing spar caps and control system account for the bulk of the airframe ADs.

Given its aesthetics and economy, the relatively rare Comanche 180 has become a desirable commodity in the light retractable market. It may be an antique, but it's a capable and useful one. If your tastes run to newer Pipers, you'll probably be more interested in the evolution of the next airplane, the Cherokee Arrow.

10 · The Piper Arrow

An Easy Step Up
for the Cherokee Pilot

On June 8, 1967, Piper received certification for a new light retractable, one designed to open up high-performance flying to the Cherokee generation—the new pilots who had grown up with Piper's Vero Beach product, the PA-28. The unpretentious little Arrow made no claim to be anything other than what it was; a gear-up version of the Cherokee 180. As such, it proved to be friendly and economical, an easy step up for anyone with the slightest familiarity with a Cherokee's characteristics.

Piper had, of course, been in the light retractable business before. Ten years earlier, it had introduced the just-reviewed Comanche 180, an airplane that found success only when a 250-hp engine was slipped under the cowling. The Arrow, by comparison, neatly filled a niche below the 260-hp Comanche B, and it soon won back a few of the customers Piper had lost to Mooney, long the sole purveyor of 180-hp retractables.

The market heated up quickly. Beech countered with the Musketeer R in 1970, Cessna introduced the Cardinal RG in 1971 and Rockwell fielded its Commander 112 in 1972. But, by the time these airplanes arrived, Piper's lead was established; none of the competitors was able to break into the market shared by the Mooney and the Arrow.

In truth, the two airplanes were hardly direct competitors. The Arrow was 17 knots slower than the Mooney at top speed, but it appealed to Piper-trained pilots with its simple systems, Cherokee-sized cabin and gentle manners. Thus, buyers seeking raw performance and economy went with the Mooney, and the ones more inclined to comfort and ease of handling opted for the gear-up Cherokee.

The 1967 appearance of the Arrow introduced several new features that were to eventually find their way into the entire Cherokee line. A stylish third side window was added, to illuminate the baggage compartment, no doubt, and the Tri-Pacer's old overhead trim crank gave way to a wheel between the front seats, a notion borrowed from the Cherokee Six. Unfortunately it proved to be much stiffer and harder to move than the ceiling-mounted crank, which could be twirled with a fingertip.

The Cherokee panel and engine controls were extensively restyled. The

The Arrow introduced a new cockpit, featuring a power quadrant, rams-horn yokes, low-set engine instruments and a trim wheel instead of an overhead crank.

The Piper Cherokee Arrow 180 was introduced in 1967 as a perfect step-up airplane for Piper Cherokee pilots.

flight instruments and engine gauges were placed in upper and lower segments of the panel, avionics were stacked on the right side and the push-pull power knobs were replaced with a flashy set of power levers in a multi-engine style quadrant, a configuration soon imitated by almost everyone except Cessna. The dowdy early-Cherokee butterfly control wheels gave way to heavy rams-horn yokes. This whole array of improvements showed up in the fixed-gear Cherokee 180D and 235C a year later.

Not Your Father's PA-28

It would be wrong to characterize the early 180-hp Arrows as Cherokee 180s with folding wheels. The engine was a fuel-injected Lycoming IO-360-B1E, in place of the fixed-gear airplanes' simpler O-360-A3A, and it twisted a constant-speed Hartzell propeller instead of the fixed-pitch Sensenich. Thus, the Arrow's engine wound up on takeoff with a 180-hp snarl, while the most the Cherokee 180 could produce at its static rpm was about 135 hp. The smaller 5.00 x 5 nose wheel, mounted nine inches farther forward, gave a more sensitive taxi feel than the 180's 6.00 x 6 tires. The open gear wells also added considerable drag when the wheels were down. Many fixed-gear Cherokee pilots were surprised by the Arrow's steep descent with the power back and its lackluster climb rate until the gear was stowed on takeoff. While the airframe was pure PA-28, the details belonged to the Arrow.

The original Arrow had this pitot head for the automatic landing gear system on the left side of the fuselage. It prevented the gear from being retracted too early and automatically extended the wheels if power was reduced at approach speed.

Among the chief virtues of the new Piper product was its simple landing gear system, powered by an electrically-driven hydraulic power pack rather than an engine-driven pump like the Aztec's, or directly by an electric motor, as in the Comanche. Moreover, Piper had rigged the gear with a mind of its own; a small pitot head jutting out of the left side of the fuselage sensed slipstream forces, commanding the power pack to automatically extend the gear if airspeed dropped below 105 mph with the power back, and to leave the gear down until climb out speed built up to 85 mph or so.

Should the gear decide not to extend, because of electrical problems or whatever, one simply dumped hydraulic pressure with a push of a lever, allowing the wheels to fall into place by gravity. Unfortunately, the pressure diaphragm in the automatic gear system deteriorates with age, causing the gear to resist honest attempts to make it retract, and the possible legal implications of this on a short-field climb out led Piper to issue a strongly-worded 1987 service bulletin to have the perfectly-valid system removed, although the request stopped short of a mandatory AD. None of the Arrows built after the late 1980s had the system installed.

The evolution of the Arrow was, at least initially, relatively subtle. One of the first changes was a 200-hp option, made available in 1969, which allowed a 100-pound increase in gross weight and made the airplane a more viable four-place machine. By 1972, the Arrow 200 was the obvious choice of the buying public; the 180-hp Arrow had disappeared, and 1973 marked the transition to the Arrow II, with a much improved airframe that was common to the rest of the PA-28 line as well. The Arrow II fuselage was stretched five inches, adding needed leg room to the rear seats and widening the door for easier boarding. The stabilator's span was increased by two feet and the wingspan was also increased by adding 12 inches to each wingtip. A dorsal fin was also added ahead of the vertical tail. The net effect of the changes in the Arrow II was a more stable airplane with more usable cabin room, although gross weight went up by only 50 pounds. A total of 1,165 180-hp Arrows were built, plus 841 200-hp versions, before upgrading to the Arrow II. In all an astounding 1,945 Arrow IIs rolled out the door.

The Arrow II was replaced in 1977 by the Arrow III, which shared the tapered wing planform previously introduced on the Warrior and Archer II. The wingspan went up to 35.5 feet, from the stubby 32-foot span used previously. Although wing area was unchanged at 170 square feet, the longer, tapered outboard wing panels improved the glide ratio and softened the old

The late-model Piper Arrow's double-tapered outer wing panels give it extra performance even at its higher gross weight.

The latest Piper Arrow has a no-nonsense all-metal panel with plenty of space for instruments and avionics. Raising and lowering the landing gear, however, is entirely the pilot's responsibility.

Hershey Bar wing's sudden stall, which sometimes led to abrupt touchdowns. Gross weight increased by another 100 pounds, to 2,750 pounds, even though the increase was more than eaten up by a heavier empty weight, particularly when full fuel was on board. As a cure for the short legs allowed by the 48 gallons in the original Cherokee tanks, 72 usable gallons were made available in the Arrow III.

One reason for the extra fuel tankage was the creation of the Turbo Arrow III, which also became available in 1977. It was identical to the normally-aspirated airplane except for the engine, a 200-hp turbocharged Continental TSIO-360-F six-cylinder engine similar to the Seneca II's powerplant. In keeping with the traditional Arrow simplicity, the Turbo III used a basic fixed-wastegate system with an overboost relief valve and a light to remind the pilot to back off the throttle; still there were no cowl flaps to forget. The Turbo Arrow's gross weight leaped to 2,900 pounds, a fairly heavy load for a 200-hp engine.

The Arrow III was only built for two years. 493 of those made were normally-aspirated and 798 were turbocharged versions. In 1979 the III was replaced by the T-tailed Arrow IV, of which about 480 were produced through 1982. The normally-aspirated Arrow IV then lay dormant as a casualty of the general aviation recession, although the Turbo Arrow IV remained in limited production into 1987, for a total run of 890 units.

The trendy T-tail of the Arrow IV was tamed by slots in the stabilator and inboard flow fences to keep the vertical fin's influence at bay. The result was a viceless airplane with few of the shortcomings of the Arrow IV's larger sibling, the T-tail Lance. I flew my first Arrow IV without so much as a verbal check-out, and I couldn't tell that the stabilator had been moved topside.

In 1988, a revitalized Piper under private ownership restarted production of a low-tailed Arrow, essentially the Arrow III but marketed without specific designation. Thus, the Arrow will doubtless claim the crown as the light retractable with the longest continuous production life.

Shopping List

As used airplanes, Arrows are good, desirable property, always in demand for personal transportation. Their closest high-performance competition has always been the Cessna 182 Skylane (the straight leg version being in roughly the same price range). Both airplanes cruise around 150 mph (130 kts), have straightforward handling characteristics for low-time pilots, and hold few surprises at annual inspection time. The big-engined Skylane burns two more gallons of fuel per hour and offers a huge cabin, but drags its feet in the wind—an inefficient and unmachismo trait.

A pre-purchase inspection can follow the usual Cherokee guidelines; the airframe is uncomplicated and has few serious airworthiness directives, although there are a host of minor-yet-required ones for your A&P to check out. The nose-gear trunnion needed modification in 1976, some stabilator fittings and tubes required inspection, and fuel tanks, which are actually part of the wing, should be noted for signs of seepage. It is important to remember that both the 200-hp Lycoming and the turbocharged Continental are highly-stressed, sophisticated powerplants, putting out a lot of power for their size, and they have a history of service problems. The difficulties of the Lycoming IO-360 center chiefly on oil pump impellers and the Bendix fuel injection system's diaphragms. The Continental has had trouble just about everywhere—cylinders, crankcases, oil pumps and magnetos—because of its harsh working environment.

The Arrow preflight follows a typical nose-to-tail pattern, checking the spinner and backing plate for cracks, propeller for nicks and security and nose gear retraction parts for cleanliness. Although there is an oil door, the upper cowling can be popped off in seconds by undoing four latches. The entire front of the Arrow is made of fiberglass, as with most PA-28s.

Fuel is easily checked by removing the caps and looking at the level's relationship to an 18-gallon tab in each tank, assuming you have the older 50-gallon system. The larger tanks have a 25-gallon tab. A sump drain is on each tank's rear inboard corner, while the fuel strainer drain sticks out of the left side of the lower cowling.

The ailerons are piano-hinged affairs, counterweighted at the outboard ends, while the flaps are the slotted, externally-hinged type. You manually extend them to 10, 25 and 40-degrees by a floor-mounted lever. Longitudinal axis rigging is accomplished by adjusting one of the flaps' up-stops. The main

The Arrow's upper cowling could be removed in seconds by unfastening four retaining clamps, allowing easy access to the IO-360 engine.

The Piper Cherokee Arrow shared the basic Cherokee 180 airframe, with nose gear located farther forward and a 5.00 x 5 tire. The new third side window and interior improvements were transferred to the 1968 Cherokee 180D.

gear hinges inboard into open wheel-wells, after the nose gear folds aft to begin the cycle. Two inches of strut extension are normal for the main gear, 2.75 inches for the nose gear. Standard 6.00 x 6 tires are used on the main gear.

The large baggage door is found behind the right wing root and folds upward where it can be pinned in place by a utilitarian web strap. This arrangement holds it out of the way of boarding passengers, while a forward hinge or gas-cylinder lift would obstruct the wing walk. Baggage capacity is 200 pounds. A 12-volt battery lives behind the baggage bin's aft bulkhead, along with the gear system. The aft tailcone should be inspected for bird nests and debris through the stabilator and trim-tab actuator openings. The trim tab is an anti-servo unit to provide feel for the all-flying tail. In early Arrows,

The 2002 New Piper Arrow incorporates the five-inch fuselage stretch and wider stabilator of the Arrow II, the tapered wing of the Arrow III and a modern panel and interior.

the rudder cannot be moved on the ground because of the nose gear's direct steering linkage; this was changed later when the tapered wing model was introduced.

Because the Arrow has been in production over several decades in varying renditions, we flew several airplanes in the course of researching this chapter. The 180-hp Arrow we tested weighed 1,520 pounds empty, so its full fuel payload capacity was 680 pounds, exactly four 170-pound standard persons. The air-conditioned 2002 Arrow, on the other hand, weighed 1,851 pounds and could carry only 475 pounds with tanks topped, owing to the 72-gallons of gas and 60-pound A/C system. However, by fueling to the 48-gallon capacity of the early airplanes and not ordering air conditioning, it could also have lifted four 170-pounders, thanks to an extra 250 pounds of gross weight and an 8-pound ramp weight allowance.

Let's Fly!

Flying the Arrow is anticlimactic. The Lycoming versions start easily, using the handbook's procedure (boost pump on, mixture rich for priming, then back to idle cutoff for cranking, returning to rich when the engine starts) Turbo Arrows are usually equipped with an optional electric priming button on the panel—a momentary high boost pump setting to persuade the Continental to keep running.

Taxiing is straightforward, except for a common tendency for new Cherokee pilots to place their feet too high on the brake pedals, where their toes mash down ineffectually on the torque tubes suspending the pedals from above. The PA-28s have always handled well in strong winds, thanks to their 10.5 foot main gear span.

Runup is done at a rather furious 2,100 or 2,300 rpm, depending on the engine, to avoid continuous operation in the red arc on the tachometer. This prohibited area encompasses 2,000 to 2,200 rpm in the 180-hp version or 2,100 to 2,350 in the 200-hp variants (an operational restriction imposed by harmonic vibrations from the combination of a large-displacement four-cylinder engine and a two-blade propeller). Retrofitted three-blade propellers are available, which eliminates the restrictions and the 2002 Arrow's McCauley prop had no placard on its tachometer.

It is important to engage the overhead door latch on the early Arrows; although no panic need result from a cracked-open door, it probably will be necessary to land and secure it. For takeoff the boost pump should be on, air conditioner off (blower can be left on) and flaps left up—although the T-tail Arrow rotates easier with one notch of flaps. For short and soft field departures a second notch of flaps are called for (25 degrees).

If you need to clear obstacles after liftoff, you must retract the landing gear as soon as possible, which requires you to outfox the early Arrow's automatic anti-retraction feature by holding up the emergency extension lever for the landing gear. This bypasses the slipstream sensor's lockout. Before 1972 one had to keep a hand on the lever continuously at lower speeds—a burdensome practice for maneuvers like stalls, short-field climbs, and especially engine-out glides. This finally prompted Piper to engineer a latch for the bypass handle, with a flashing light to show that it was engaged. Some owners of pre-1972 Arrows whittled out a curved block of wood to keep the lever up, an example of mankind's ingenuity at defeating safety features.

Considerable torque is noticeable when power is advanced, but is easily handled with right rudder. The nose can be raised at around 40 knots on rough fields, using full-up stabilator. However, normally rotation begins at 50 knots or so, and liftoff around 65 knots. V_X with flaps down is 69 to 72 knots, depending on model year, or 72 to 79 knots with flaps up. Best rate of climb comes at around 85 to 90 knots, with the higher-gross models requiring more speed. About 800 fpm will typically be seen as a sea-level climb rate. The landing gear has a 109-knot maximum retraction speed, not usually encountered as a problem.

Transitioning into level cruise is not complicated by having cowl flaps to close, but it is a good time to re-check that you turned the boost pump off during departure. The usual Cherokee fuel management is needed, due to the tanks' long arm from the fuselage centerline. To keep balanced laterally, you should switch tanks after the first half-hour, switch again after one hour and continue switching every hour thereafter, so you are never more than a half-hour out of balance between tanks. The rudder trim bungee adjusts yaw forces for long climbs.

Cockpit visibility is generally good, although the fat wingtips obstruct the view when a wing is raised, and the low window line requires some ducking to see while the aircraft is in a right turn. Roll rates are not exactly aerobatic, but one must remember that this is a cruiser, not a sports car. The short stabilator of the first Arrows results in a little control wheel "hunting," small fore and aft movements in rough air, a harmless characteristic that keeps the pilot awake. It has the usual Cherokee drawbacks of the single door, some deterioration of the economy-class interior trim, seats that age quickly and handling that is somewhat lackluster. But, the Arrow carries a good load, thanks to its light-weight structure, and it demands little of its pilot. The safety landing gear is a good feature if it is still operational, although it is not foolproof. I watched a near belly-landing one day when an Arrow pilot suffered electrical failure and had no gear warning horn or lights to tell him his pump wasn't operating. His final warning, a very unArrow-like float in the flare, caught his attention just in time.

I asked my local A&P/IA for his advice on buying a used Arrow, and he simply said, "If you like the color and you can afford it, buy it." So, have a trusted mechanic look over your prospective purchase for obvious flaws, and you'll enjoy the Arrow's gear-up cruising. As with all the Cherokees, Arrow flying is good, simple fun; retracting the gear just makes it more so.

11 · The Commander 112
Biggest Light Retractable

American industrial giant Rockwell International entered the general aviation field in the late 1950s with the acquisition of Aero Design & Engineering, builders of business twins. Attempting to broaden the Commander line with single-engine airplanes, Rockwell made further acquisitions in the 1960s, including the Volaire fixed-gear four-seater and Meyers high-performance retractable. Despite its best efforts to bring these diverse products into a cohesive whole, by the end of the decade it was evident that Rockwell needed to design a new line of airplanes from scratch.

Rockwell's impressive design team included Karl Bergey, who had worked on the certification of Piper's Cherokee line. The goal was to create a Rockwell airframe that could be adapted to a variety of uses, as Cessna and Piper had done. The first production model was to be a light retractable, the Commander 112, using a 200-hp Lycoming IO-360; a 180-hp Commander 111 fixed-gear version of the 112 was certified along with the 112 on June 1, 1972, but

At mid to upper altitudes, the Commander 112TC combines economical operation with a 135-knot cruise. The airplane's modern design and spacious interior make it a desirable commodity on the used market.

The Commander 112 is a large-cabin airplane offering moderate performance with a comfortable ride. Non-turbocharged airplanes with the shorter 32.75-foot wingspan handle turbulence better but don't perform as well at altitude as this 112TC.

never marketed. Subsequent follow-on models included the 260-hp 114 and a turbocharged 112TC, and there were plans to build a light twin version, but by 1980 Rockwell's bold attempt had ended. A total of 534 Commander 112s were built from 1972 through 1977, plus 191 turbocharged 112TCs.

A Large Small Retractable

Market conditions notwithstanding, the Commander 112 was and is a basically sound airplane. Rockwell's design team realized it couldn't just offer another Mooney Super 21 or Piper Arrow; the 112 needed to have things other airplanes did not. The result was a wide, comfortable cabin with two big doors, costing a bit of speed but adding living space. A cruciform tail promised less vibration by putting the stabilizer above the propwash and soft trailing-link landing gear created effortless landings.

When Rockwell sprang the 200-hp Commander 112 on the market in 1972, it sold moderately well after an increase in useful load. Originally, 125 straight-112s were sold with a maximum gross weight of 2,550 pounds and 48-gallons of fuel; the 1974 change to a 112A offered a gross of 2,650 pounds and 68-gallon optional tanks, of which 344 were built. The highly-desirable final-edition, the 1977 112B, had the extended wing span of the turbocharged 112TC and a gross weight of 2,800 pounds; only 45 were produced. Unfortunately, the biggest-is-best American taste favored the 114 that was fielded in 1976, and the 112 went away after 1977.

In the meantime, Rockwell had discovered an unserved market niche, the need for a modestly-powered turbocharged widebody single. While everybody else was concentrating on big 300-hp turbo cruisers that burned 17 to 18 gph, Rockwell brought out the 112TC in 1976, certificated on April 27. This airplane offered a generously-sized cabin with a four-cylinder Lycoming TO-360 that could produce 210-hp with heavy breathing, thereby saving 5 gph fuel flow versus the bigger planes. Gross weight was up to a hefty 2,850 pounds.

The Perfect First Plane

As an example of the best of the small Commanders, Dennis Shy of St. Louis, Missouri, was willing to share his Commander 112TC with us. As Shy's first airplane, the Commander did all that he expected of it. Comfort and travel capability were high on his list; the turbocharger, he said, was just a bonus. Shy bought the airplane before he had a private license and he expected to keep it for a while, so he brought it up to date with an engine overhaul, new radios and a fresh interior and exterior. He likes to follow the NASCAR weekend race circuit, a good mission for the 112TC. In addition, Shy's company does commercial printing jobs over a wide area, so he had more than one reason to want a simple, easy-to-operate traveling airplane. The 112TC has met his needs.

Stem to Stern

The Commander 112TC uses a carbureted TO-360 Lycoming with a factory-installed RayJay turbocharger, instead of the fuel-injected IO-360 more normally seen in light retractables, and it is only slightly related to the regular O-360 engines, as Shy found out when he took his airplane down for overhaul. Rebuilding costs $6,000 more and comes 200 hours earlier than with the IO-360. The parts are different, more akin to the turbocharged Piper Navajo's TIO-540 and 541 powerplants. Even without fuel injection, there's no chance of carburetor icing with the dragon's breath of the turbocharger feeding the carburetor, and any power loss from the use of a carburetor can be made up by boosting the intake manifold's pressure.

The TO-360 is a somewhat upside-down powerplant; the induction system is underneath the engine and the exhaust manifold is on the top, where it feeds the turbo through a fixed wastegate and exhausts through a large single tailpipe on the right rear of the engine. Cooling air moves in an updraft path, from the lower part of the nosecap over the cylinders and into the pressure plenum above the engine. One learns not to rest one's hand on the upper cowling after shutdown, and to be careful with the oil access door in the top cowl. An inlet on the right side of the cowling feeds the induction air filter and a similar opening on the left side goes to the oil cooler. Adjustable cowl flaps are found under the cowling. The upper portion of the cowling is removable by simply popping open two latches on each side. A single landing light is located under the spinner.

The landing gear system is rugged and simple. The main gear features 11-inch trailing-link shock struts for easy touchdowns, with 7.00 x 6 tires. Large open wheel wells are needed to capture the inward-folding wheels and struts. A 5.00 x 5 tire is on the nose gear, retracting straight aft and up. Powered and held in position by hydraulic pressure from an electrically-driven power pack, the wheels can be extended without assistance by simply opening a valve to dump the pressure, which allows them to free-fall and lock down.

The Commander's massive trailing-link main gear struts fold away into open wells under the wing and are fitted with oversize 7.00 x 6 tires.

The Commander's relatively small wings are tapered in planform, using slotted flaps for added lift and drag. Beaded skins aft of the spar add stiffness and flush riveting is employed forward of the main spar. The 112TC had an extra 17 inches added to each wingtip, outboard of the ailerons, adding 12 square feet of wing area to enhance climb and high-altitude performance over the standard Commander 112. The fuel system consists of 35-gallon integral tanks in each wing, with 24-gallon reduced-fuel tabs in the filler necks, which are equipped with anti-siphon flappers as part of the later FAR Part 23 certification required of the 112. Anti-collision strobes housed in the wingtips and tail supplement the red flashing beacon atop the tailfin. The pitot tube is on the left wing, along with the stall warning vane; static ports are on the sides of the aft fuselage. Leading edge air inlets near the wing root feed lower vents in the cabin.

Because the Commanders feature doors on both sides of the fuselage, a courtesy light near each boarding step illuminates the aft wing walk, actuated by a push button on the left side of the fuselage for a 3-minute duration. A hot-wired light in the baggage compartment comes on when the door is opened on the left side of the fuselage. A 12-volt battery is in the aft tailcone, along with the ELT and landing gear powerpack.

The cruciform tail design was chosen as a compromise, a way to raise the stabilizer above the turbulent slipstream but avoid the handling and structural problems associated with a T-tail. Once you learn to wait for a rotation speed of around 70 knots on takeoff, the tail works well. The empennage shows the same beaded metal work found on the wings along with an air inlet on the tail for ducts in the overhead cabin. A generous ventral fin under the belly enhances yaw stability.

After the dormant Commander design was sold to Gulfstream in the 1990s, three service-related problems showed up, requiring compliance with Airworthiness Directives for continued airworthiness. These were related to the vertical tail/fuselage attachment, the main landing gear's trunnion on the wing spar and the front seat adjustment rails. An extensive AD-compliance program was undertaken in the 1990s to beef up all three of these areas, as a joint effort of Gulfstream American and a restarted Commander Aircraft that had resumed 114 production. At this point, the work has presumably been done on all aircraft still in the field; check the airframe log for compliance with ADs 90-4-7, 88-5-6 and 77-16-9. Extra rivets on the vertical fin show where the work was performed.

The Commander's cruciform tail design, using beaded skins, placed the horizontal stabilizer above the propeller wake.

A Nice Place for Traveling

We were ready to head upstairs to check out the Commander 112TC's performance, so we mounted our respective wing walks and settled into the sumptuously-refurbished interior. With the upholstery, paint and latest avionics enhancements, the airplane looked brand new. A Garmin GNS430 navigation system was the centerpiece, enhanced by the GNL49 weather datalink, a Garmin Mode S transponder, Bendix/King KX155 navcomm, S-Tec 55 autopilot pitch module to supplement the standard Century IIB single-axis autopilot and a PS Engineering PCD-7100R entertainment system, along with the PMA-7000CD audio-panel/intercom.

The interior and gear didn't add as much to the empty weight as we expected. At 1,805 pounds empty, we could carry full tanks and four standard 170-pound persons, assuming at least a half-gallon of fuel would be burned before takeoff. Given the normal 12–13 gph fuel burn, full tanks aren't always needed. However, a 2,620-pound zero-fuel weight restriction means that 38

The beautiful Commander panel shares the cabin's width, offering plenty of space for equipment. The central console between the seats has fuel, trim and power functions at the pilot's elbow.

gallons may as well be in the tanks for departure, since the 230 pounds to reach maximum takeoff weight can't go in the cabin.

The cabin's roomy 50-inch width allows for a center console between the front seats, containing the fuel selector, elevator trim and power handles. There is a "both" fuel tanks selection, rare in low-wing airplanes, as well as left/right options. The rudder trim knob is under the left subpanel and the cowl flap and wing flap controls are on the center panel.

Starting is carburetor-simple, with mixture rich and boost pump on, followed by priming and/or throttle pumping prior to twisting the key. The tall seating allows for a good view over the nose and the straight-up nose-gear strut provides excellent taxi control. Pre-takeoff checks include a runup at 2,000 rpm for the mags and prop, setting flaps to 10 degrees, switching boost pump on, and checking cowl flaps open, upper door latches secure and storm windows closed (although they can be opened up to 130 knots).

Making Boost

The 112TC has no wastegate controller other than the pilot's right arm, so one brings in about 36 inches and waits for the remainder of the 41 inches of allowable boost to build up during the takeoff roll. We were off at 70 knots in about 2,000 feet of runway. Once gear and flaps were up we observed an 800-fpm climb rate at 85 knots; Shy says he cruise-climbs at 650 fpm up through 10,000 feet, using 100 knots. One benefit of the turbocharger is the ability to climb at a steady rate all the way to its critical altitude, which seems to be at about 13,000 feet.

Leveling at 3,500 feet MSL, we set up 35 inches m.p. and 2,450 rpm, (about 75% power), and settled in at an indicated airspeed of 125 knots burning 13 gph. This produced a true airspeed of 135 knots, at a density altitude of slightly over 5,000 feet. For a long-range cruise to simulate stretching fuel with a tailwind, we used 30 inches to achieve 118 knots IAS, a TAS of 127 knots on a fuel burn of 11 gph. The beamy 112 is no speed wagon, because Rockwell wanted to provide comfort and IFR stability with a large airframe, but its cruise numbers aren't too shabby, particularly at altitude where drag is reduced.

The 112TC handles like a transport, staying right on track when left to its own devices, and Shy finds it to be an excellent instrument platform. We slowed down to 80 knots for some slow-flight testing, still under full control, then went to idle power to see what the stall was like. We found a warning horn at 74 knots but the stall itself was delayed to about 60 knots in clean configuration. With gear and flaps deployed, we heard no stall warning until reaching 62 knots and the full break occurred at 54 knots.

At mid to upper altitudes, the Commander 112TC combines economical operation with a 135-knot cruise. A modern design and great interior keep it in demand on the used market.

Thus emboldened, we headed back to the airport and extended the landing gear for a landing. The gear can be dropped up to 130 knots and once it is down, the airplane can be dived to 180 knots if needed. As much as 20 degrees of flap can be deployed at 150 knots or less, with 5 degrees more permitted after reaching 120 knots and the full 35 degrees allowed below 109 knots. We flew our final approach at 78 knots, a fairly conservative addition to 1.3 V_{SO}. Shy has found that the rudder's power can be enhanced for crosswind control by adding a bit of throttle just prior to touchdown. We floated to the mid-field point to minimize taxi and braked to a halt in about 1,700 feet. As with most 200-hp retractables, the 112TC is able to land in less space than can be matched by the takeoff and initial climb, although the turbocharger helps to even the score at high elevation airports.

Before shut-down, Shy likes to wait for the CHT to drop and then start climbing again from residual heat in the cowling. He also parks with the fuel in "off" to prevent leakage from a low tank.

The overall impression we came away with is of a quality, solid-flying airplane, a good way to tour the country and arrive refreshed, thanks to the extra elbow room. While it's doubtful that any more small-engine Commanders will ever be built, the few used ones on the market are in demand.

Appendix
Specification Tables

Mooney Mark 20, 20A, 21 and Ranger

	M20	M20A	M20B	M20C
Price				
Introductory, std. equipment	$12,500	$14,750	$15,995	$15,995
Specifications				
Wingspan, feet	35.0	35.0	35.0	35.0
Wing area, square feet	167	167	167	167
Length, feet	23.2	23.2	23.2	23.2
Height, feet	8.4	8.4	8.4	8.4
Wheel track, feet	9.1	9.1	9.1	9.1
Wheel base, feet	6.0	6.0	6.0	6.0
Maximum gross weight, pounds	2,450	2,450	2,450	2,575
Empty weight, standard, pounds	1,415	1,440	1,525	1,525
Useful load, standard, pounds	1,035	1,010	925	1,050
Wing loading, lbs/sq. ft.	14.7	14.7	14.7	15.4
Power loading, lbs/hp	16.3	13.6	13.6	14.3
Fuel capacity, useful, gallons	50	50	48	48
Baggage capacity, pounds	120	120	120	120
Engine				
Lycoming 4-cylinder, normally-aspirated, carbureted, horizontally opposed	O-320A	O-360-A1A	O-360-A1A	O-360-1A1
	150 hp	180 hp	180 hp	180 hp
Recommended TBO, hours	2,000	2,000	2,000	2,000
Propeller				
Two-blade, constant-speed, all metal	76 in	74 in	74 in	74 in

Performance

Maximum speed, mph	171	190	190	185
Cruise, 75% power, mph	165	180	180	180
Range, maximum, no reserve, s.mi	1,000	1,075	1,130	1,031
Cruise speed, max range power, mph	150	160	165	122
Stall speed, gear and flaps down, mph	57	57	57	57
Rate of climb, sea level, fpm	900	1,150	1,150	1,010
Service ceiling, feet	17,200	20,000	18,500	18,000
Takeoff ground roll, feet	850	775	775	815
Landing ground roll, feet	600	600	600	550

The Mooney M20C, also called the Ranger, was one of the most popular Mooney models, produced from 1962 to 1978. The basic Mooney, it was powered by the 180-hp O-360 engine.

Mooney Super 21, Executive, Statesman, 201

	M20E	M20F	M20G	M20J
Price				
Introductory, std. equipment	$18,450	$21,995	$18,790	$41,200
Specifications				
Wingspan, feet	35.0	35.0	35.0	36.1
Wing area, square feet	167	167	167	167
Length, feet	23.2	24.3	24.3	24.7
Height, feet	8.4	8.4	8.4	8.3
Wheel track, feet	9.1	9.1	9.1	9.1
Wheel base, feet	6.0	6.0	6.0	6.0
Maximum gross weight, pounds	2,575	2,740	2,525	2,740
Empty weight, standard, pounds	1,560	1,622	1,585	1,640
Useful load, standard, pounds	1,050	1,118	940	1,100
Wing loading, lbs/sq. ft.	15.4	16.4	15.1	16.4
Power loading, lbs/hp	12.9	13.7	14.0	13.7
Fuel capacity, usable, gallons	52	64	52	64
Baggage capacity, pounds	120	130	130	130
Engine				
Lycoming 4-cylinder, normally-aspirated, horizontally opposed	IO-360A1A	IO-360-A1A	O-360-A1D	IO-360-1B6D
	200 hp	200 hp	180 hp	200 hp
Recommended TBO, hours	2,000	2,000	2,000	2,000
Propeller				
Two-blade, constant-speed, all metal	74 in	74 in	74 in	74 in

Performance

Maximum speed, mph	197	197	178	201
Cruise, 75% power, mph	187	187	169	195
Range, maximum, no reserve, s.mi	1,024	1,400	925	1,295
Cruise speed, max range power, mph	168	168	155	174
Stall speed, gear and flaps down, mph	57	64	57	61
Rate of climb, sea level, fpm	1,120	1,080	875	1,030
Service ceiling, feet	19,500	17,900	17,000	18,800
Takeoff ground roll, feet	760	879	815	970
Landing ground roll, feet	595	785	595	800

Mooney's M20E, a.k.a. the Super 21 or Chaparral, combined the short fuselage of the M20C with Lycoming's 200-hp IO-360 engine. It was stretched to create the M20F Executive that ultimately became the 201.

1947 Beechcraft Bonanza

Price

New, standard equipment	$8,945

Specifications

Wingspan	32.83 feet
Wing area	177.6 sq. ft.
Length	25.17 feet
Height	6.51 feet
Wheel track	9.58 feet
Wheel base	7.02 feet
Landing gear type	retractable, tricycle
Tire size, mains	6.50 x 8
Tire size, nose	5.00 x 5
Seats	4

Weights and loading

Maximum gross weight	2,550 lbs
Empty weight, standard	1,490 lbs
Empty weight, as tested	1,684 lbs
Useful load, standard	1,060 lbs
Useful load, as tested	866 lbs
Wing loading	14.35 lb/sq. ft.
Power loading	15.45 lbs/hp
Fuel capacity, total/useful	40/34 gal
Baggage capacity	120 lbs

Engine

Continental E-185-1 six-cylinder, 471 CID, normally-aspirated, carbureted, horizontally-opposed, 185 hp for takeoff at 2,300 rpm (1 minute), 165 hp max continuous power at 2,050 rpm. Recommended TBO 1,500 hours.

Propeller

Beech 215 2-blade adjustable pitch, electrically controlled, 88-inch diameter

Performance

Maximum speed	184 mph
Cruise speed, 70% power, 10,000 feet	175 mph
Range, maximum, no reserve	750 s.m.
Stall speed, flaps up	59 mph
Stall speed, flaps down	46 mph
Rate of climb, sea level	950 fpm
Service ceiling	18,000 feet
Takeoff ground roll, 10 knot headwind	425 feet (factory specs)
Landing ground roll, 10 knot headwind	315 feet (factory specs)

First built in 1947, Walter Beech's famous Bonanza was originally a lightweight low-powered airplane, with a gross weight and horsepower similar to the Mooney, Piper and Cessna light retractables that followed it.

Beech Musketeer Super R, Sierra B24R, C24R

	A24R	B24R	C24R
Price			
Introductory, standard equipment, f.a.f	$24,950	$25,795	$39,000
Specifications			
Wingspan, feet	32.75	32.75	32.75
Wing area, square feet	146	146	146
Length, feet	25.75	25.75	25.75
Height, feet	8.08	8.08	8.08
Wheel track, feet	12.67	12.67	12.67
Wheel base, feet	6.08	6.08	6.08
Maximum gross weight, lbs	2,750	2,750	2,750
Empty weight, standard, lbs	1,618	1,617	1,711
Useful load, standard, lbs	1,132	1,133	1,039
Wing loading, lbs/sq. ft.	18.84	18.84	18.84
Power loading, lbs/hp	13.75	13.75	13.75
Fuel capacity, useful, gallons	58.8	52.0	57.2
Baggage capacity, lbs	270	270	270

Engine

Lycoming IO-360, 4-cylinder, normally aspirated fuel-injected,
horizontally-opposed, 200 hp at 2,700 rpm.
Recommended TBO 1,800 hours (orig. 1,200 hours)

Propeller

Two-blade, constant speed, all metal
   McCauley 2D34-C9/78FBM-1.5, 76.5 in.
   Hartzell HC-M2YR-1BF/F7666A-2R, 74 in.
   Hartzell HC-M2YR-1BF/F7666A, 76 in.

Performance

Maximum speed	148 kts	140 kts	145 kts
Maximum cruise speed	141 kts	131 kts	137 kts
Cruise, 75% power	122 kts	111 kts	115 kts
Range, 75% power, with reserve	617 nm	561 nm	646 nm
Range, 55% power, with reserve	668 nm	593 nm	686 nm
Stall speed, gear and flaps up	65 kts	65 kts	65 kts
Stall speed, gear and flaps down	57 kts	55 kts	60 kts
Rate of climb, sea level	862 fpm	891 fpm	927 fpm
Service ceiling, feet	14,350	14,342	15,385
Takeoff ground roll, feet	1,100	1,169	1,063
Takeoff over 50-foot obstacle, feet	1,630	1,804	1,561
Landing over 50-foot obstacle, feet	1,330	1,519	1,462
Landing ground roll, feet	760	803	816

Evolving from Beech's Musketeer line of light airplanes, the Sierra became a sturdy, dependable traveling platform. The C24R was the last of the line, built from 1977 to 1983.

1971 Cessna 177RG Cardinal RG

Price

New, standard equipment	$24,795

Specifications

Wingspan	35.5 feet
Wing area	174 sq. ft.
Length	27.25 feet
Height	8.58 feet
Wheel track	7.83 feet
Wheel base	7.5 feet
Landing gear type	retractable, tricycle
Tire size, mains	15 x 6.00-6
Tire size, nose	5.00 x 5
Seats	4

Weights and loading

Maximum gross weight	2,800 lbs
Empty weight, standard	1,630 lbs
Empty weight, as tested	1,772 lbs
Useful load, standard	1,170 lbs
Useful load, as tested	1,028 lbs
Wing loading	16.1 lbs/sq. ft.
Power loading	14 lbs/hp
Fuel capacity, total/useful	51/50 gal.
Baggage capacity	120 lbs

Engine

Lycoming IO-360-A1B6, four-cylinder horizontally-opposed, normally-aspirated, fuel-injected, 200 BHP at 2,700 rpm, recommended TBO 2,000 hours

Propeller

McCauley B2D34C206/78TA, two-blade, constant-speed, 78-inch diameter

Performance

Maximum speed	153 kts
Cruise speed, 75% cruise power, 7,000 feet	144 kts
Range, maximum cruise power, no reserve	665 nm
Cruise speed, economy power, 10,000 feet	117 kts
Range, economy power, no reserve	778 nm
Stall speed, flaps up	57 kts
Stall speed, flaps down	50 kts
Rate of climb, sea level	860 fpm
Service ceiling	16,900 feet
Takeoff ground roll	890 feet
Takeoff over 50-foot obstacle	1,585 feet
Landing over 50-foot obstacle	1,350 feet
Landing ground roll	730 feet

As a lightweight alternative to the big Centurion, Cessna's Cardinal RG offered a big cabin, excellent speed and unmatched visibility. The retractable-gear version actually outsold the fixed-gear model.

1980 Cessna Cutlass RG

Price

New, standard equipment	$43,395

Specifications

Wingspan	36 feet (with strobes)
Wing area	174 sq. ft.
Length	27.42 feet
Height	8.79 feet
Wheel track	8.5 feet
Wheel base	5.20 feet
Landing gear type	retractable, tri-cycle
Tire size, mains	15 x 6.00-6
Tire size, nose	5.00-5
Seats	4

Weights and loading

Maximum ramp weight	2,658 lbs
Maximum gross weight	2,650 lbs
Empty weight, standard	1,558 lbs
Empty weight, as tested	1,666 lbs
Useful load, standard	1,100 lbs
Useful load, as tested	992 lbs
Wing loading	15.2 lbs/sq. ft.
Power loading	14.7 lbs/hp
Fuel capacity, total/useful	66/62 gal.
Baggage capacity	200 lbs

Engine

Lycoming O-360-F1A6, four-cylinder, horizontally-opposed, direct-drive, normally-aspirated, carbureted, 361 CID, 180 hp at 2,700 rpm. Recommended TBO 2,000 hours

Propeller

McCauley B2D34C220/80VHA-3.5, two-blade, constant-speed, 76.5 inch diameter

Performance

Maximum speed	145 kts
Cruise speed, maximum cruise power, 9,000 feet	140 kts
Range, maximum cruise power, with reserve	720 nm
Cruise speed, economy power, 10,000 feet	120 kts
Range, economy power, with reserve	830 nm
Stall speed, flaps up	54 kts
Stall speed, flaps down	50 kts
Rate of climb, sea level	800 fpm
Service ceiling	16,800 feet
Takeoff ground roll	940 feet
Takeoff over 50-foot obstacle	1,675 feet
Landing over 50-foot obstacle	1,340 feet
Landing ground roll	625 feet

There's no mistaking the Cutlass RG's origins. With fixed landing gear appended, it would look and fly exactly like the Cessna Skyhawk, the most popular airplane ever built.

1980 Lake LA-4-200 Buccaneer

Price

New, standard equipment	$74,060

Specifications

Wingspan	38 feet
Wing area	170 sq. ft.
Length	24.92 feet
Height	9.33 feet
Wheel track	11.17 feet
Wheel base	6.83 feet
Landing gear type	retractable, tricycle
Tire size, mains	6.00 x 6
Tire size, nose	5.00 x 5
Seats	4

Weights and loading

Maximum gross weight	2,690 lbs
Empty weight, standard	1,555 lbs
Empty weight, as tested	1,660 lbs
Useful load, standard	1,135 lbs
Useful load, as tested	1,030 lbs
Wing loading	15.82 lb/sq. ft.
Power loading	13.45 lb/hp
Fuel capacity, total/usable	55/54 gal.
Baggage capacity	200 lbs

Engine

Lycoming IO-360-A1B four-cylinder opposed, fuel-injected, direct-drive, normally-aspirated, air-cooled, 200-hp at 2,700 rpm, recommended TBO 2,000 hours

Propeller

Hartzell HC-C2YK-1BL/L7666A-2 two-blade, constant-speed, 74-inch diameter

Performance

Maximum speed	135 kts
Cruise speed, 75% power	127 kts
Range, 75% power, no reserve	715 n.mi.
Stall speed, flaps up	45 kts
Stall speed, flaps down	39 kts
Rate of climb, sea level	1,200 fpm
Service ceiling	14,700 feet
Takeoff ground roll	600 feet
Landing ground roll	475 feet

The Lake Buccaneer opens up a whole world of alternative landing sites with its ability to touch down on water as well as land. A marginal performer with four aboard, it's a fine waterbird for two persons and their gear.

Piper PA-24 Comanche 180

Price

New, standard equipment, f.a.f.	$14,500

Specifications

Wingspan	36 feet
Wing area	178 sq. ft.
Length	24.7 feet
Height	7.3 feet
Wheel track	9.8 feet
Wheel base	6.5 feet
Landing gear type	retractable, tricycle
Tire size, mains	6.00 x 6
Tire size, nose	6.00 x 6
Seats	4

Weights and loading

Maximum gross weight	2,550 lbs
Empty weight, standard	1,475 lbs
Empty weight, as tested	1,567 lbs
Useful load, standard	1,075 lbs
Useful load, as tested	983 lbs
Wing loading	14.3 lbs/sq. ft.
Power loading	14.2 lbs/hp
Fuel capacity	60 gal.
Baggage capacity	200 lbs

Engine

Lycoming O-360-A1A four-cylinder opposed, air-cooled, normally-aspirated, carbureted, 180-hp at 2,700 rpm. Recommended TBO 2,000 hours

Propeller

Hartzell HC92K8D two-blade constant-speed, 74-inch diameter

Performance

Maximum speed	145 kts
Cruise speed, 75% power, 8,000 feet	139 kts
Range, 75% cruise power, no reserve	835 nm
Cruise speed, 55% power, 12,000 feet	117 kts
Range, 55% power, no reserve	1,110 n.m.
Stall speed, gear and flaps up	55 kts
Stall speed, flaps down	50 kts
Rate of climb, sea level	910 fpm
Service ceiling	18,500 feet
Takeoff ground roll	750 feet
Takeoff over 50-foot obstacle	2,240 feet
Landing over 50-foot obstacle	1,025 feet
Landing ground roll	600 feet

Long, lean and appealing, Piper's Comanche does a fine job with 180 horsepower as long as the weight limits are respected. The International Comanche Society provides much-needed support for its members and should be a must-join priority for prospective buyers.

Piper Arrow

	Arrow 180	Arrow 200	Arrow II
	PA-28R-180	PA-28R-200	PA-28R-200
Years produced	1967–1971	1969–1971	1972–1976
Introductory base price	$16,900	$18,500	$24,200

Specifications

	Arrow 180	Arrow 200	Arrow II
Wingspan, feet	30	30	32
Wing area, square feet	160	160	170
Length, feet	24.2	24.2	24.6
Height, feet	8	8	8
Wheel track, feet	10.5	10.5	10.5
Wheel base, feet	7.4	7.4	7.8
Gross weight, lbs	2,500	2,600	2,650
Empty weight, std, lbs	1,380	1,459	1,523
Useful load, std, lbs	1,120	1,141	1,127
Wing loading, lbs/sq.ft	15.6	16.3	15.6
Power loading, lbs/hp	13.89	13.0	13.25
Fuel capacity, usable, gallons	48	48	48
Baggage capacity, lbs	200	200	200
Lycoming engine	IO-360-B1E	IO-360-C1C	IO-360-C1C
Horsepower	180	200	200
Recommended TBO, hours	2,000	2,000	2,000
Propeller, 2-blade, constant-speed, inches diameter	76	74	74

Performance

	Arrow 180	Arrow 200	Arrow II
Maximum speed, kts	148	153	153
Cruise, 75% power, kts	141	144	143
Range, 55% power, nm, no/res.	862	825	782
Cruise, 55% power, kts	130	134	130
Stall speed, gear and flaps down, kts	53	56	56
Rate of climb, s.l., fpm	875	910	900
Service ceiling, feet	15,000	16,000	15,000
Takeoff ground roll, feet	820	770	770
Landing ground roll, feet	776	780	780

Piper Arrow

	Arrow III	Arrow IV	New Piper Arrow
	PA-28R-201	PA-28RT-201	PA-28R
Years Produced	1977–1978	1979–1982	1988–present
Introductory base price	$37,850	$44,510	$114,300

Specifications

	Arrow III	Arrow IV	New Piper Arrow
Wingspan, feet	35.33	35.33	35.4
Wing area, square feet	170	170	170
Length, feet	24.6	27	24.7
Height, feet	8	8.3	7.9
Wheel track, feet	10.47	10.47	10.47
Wheel base, feet	7.86	7.86	7.86
Gross weight, lbs	2,750	2,750	2,750
Empty weight, std, lbs	1,585	1,637	1,612
Useful load, std, lbs	1,165	1,113	1,138
Wing loading, lbs/sq.ft.	16.2	16.2	16.18
Power loading, lbs/hp	13.75	13.75	13.75
Fuel capacity, usable, gallons	72	72	72
Baggage capacity, lbs	200	200	200
Lycoming engine	IO-360-C1C6	IO-360-C1C6	IO-360-C1C6
Horsepower	200	200	200
Recommended TBO, hours	2,000	2,000	2,000
Propeller, two-blade, constant-speed, inches diameter	76	76	76

Performance

	Arrow III	Arrow IV	New Piper Arrow
Maximum speed, kts	152	149	145
Cruise, 75% power, kts	143	143	137
Cruise, 55% power, kts	128	128	125
Range, 55% power, nm, w/res.	935	935	880
Stall speed, gear and flaps down, kts	55	55	55
Rate of climb, s.l., fpm	831	831	831
Service ceiling, feet	16,200	16,200	16,000
Takeoff ground roll, feet	1,025	1,025	1,025
Landing ground roll, feet	615	615	615

1976 Rockwell Commander 112TC

Price

New, standard equipment, f.a.f.	$42,900

Specifications

Wingspan	35.58 feet
Wing area	163.8 sq. ft.
Length	25.42 feet
Height	8.42 feet
Wheel track	10.67 feet
Wheel base	6.62 feet
Landing gear type	retractable, tricycle
Tire size, mains	7.00 x 6
Tire size, nose	5.00 x 5
Seats	4

Weights and loading

Maximum gross weight	2,850 lbs
Maximum zero fuel weight	2,620 lbs
Empty weight, standard	1,769 lbs
Empty weight, as tested	1,805 lbs
Useful load, standard	1,081 lbs
Useful load, as tested	1,045 lbs
Wing loading	17.4 lb/sq. ft.
Power loading	13.57 lb/hp
Fuel capacity, usable	68 gal.
Baggage capacity	200 lbs

Engine

Lycoming TO-360-C1A6D four-cylinder opposed, air-cooled, direct-drive, turbocharged, carbureted, 210-hp at 42 inches m.p. & 2,575 rpm, recommended TBO 1,800 hours

Propeller

Hartzell HC-E2YR-1BF/F8467-7R, two-blade, constant-speed, 77 inch diameter

Performance

Maximum speed	164 kts
Cruise speed, 75% power, 8,000 feet	135 kts
Cruise speed, 55% power, 8,000 feet	129 kts
Range, 75% power, with reserve	640 n.mi.
Range, 55% power, with reserve	923 n.mi.
Stall speed, flaps and gear up	56 kts
Stall speed, flaps and gear down	51 kts
Rate of climb, sea level	888 fpm
Service ceiling (maximum certificated altitude)	20,000 feet
Takeoff ground roll	1,250 feet
Takeoff over 50-foot obstacle	1,800 feet
Landing ground roll	740 feet
Landing over 50-foot obstacle	1,240 feet

Rockwell's Commander 112 represented a clean-sheet approach to a new series of lightplanes, first marketed as a 200-hp retractable. It offered a huge cabin and met the latest certification standards of FAR Part 23.

Chronology of the Cessna Cardinal RG

1971 The first Cardinal RG; 51 gallons total fuel capacity, white sidewall tires, boarding steps below doors. New Cessna safety features included front seat shoulder harness, padded glareshield and door posts. Base price $24,795

1972 New propeller blade profile improves cruise speed from 166 mph to 171 mph, climb rate from 860 fpm to 925 fpm. Boarding steps were replaced by step-pad on top of gear leg, jackpoint standard on gear leg, gray instrument panel cover attached with hook-and-loop fasteners, larger control wheel grips. Base price $25,995

1973 Larger 61 gallon fuel system standard, cowling nosecap streamlined, secondary door latching pin added, four-way fuel selector added, new hydraulic downlock in gear system. Base price $25,995 again

1974 Improved landing gear actuation; gear switch changed to pilot-actuated handle directly to powerpack's valve. Better seats, increased heater output in rear cabin with adjustments, trays above door for shoulder harness when not in use, replacing wire clips used previously. Marker beacon lights downsized for more panel space, stabilator abrasion boots available for tail. Base price $26,255

1975 Shelf added to aft wall of baggage compartment, bump plates added to protect door frame when striker bolt is extended. Inertial reel shoulder harness available. Quick drains made standard, baffles in nose section boosts heating and ventilation, door hinges strengthened. Cardinal RG II package became available at $37,495, Cardinal base price $30,900

1976 Marker beacon receiver combined with audio panel, new style instrument panel without "hump" on pilot's side increased room for avionics and instruments. Primary airspeed callouts changed from mph to knots. Base price $35,550

1977 Lower panel incorporated energy-absorbing structure, fuel selector mechanism changed to match rest of line, vernier mixture control knob added. Base price $39,950

1978 Final year of Cardinal production, terminated on August 14, 1978, after 1,314 units, plus 176 F177RGs built in Reims, France. The 14-volt electrical system changed to 28-volt system, gear retraction time decreased from 12 seconds to 6 seconds, new hydraulic power pack, avionics master switch standard. Base price $43,950